Reach FOR THE Skai

Reach for the Skai

FOR THE

HOW TO INSPIRE, EMPOWER, AND CLAPBACK

SKAI JACKSON

CROWN BOOKS FOR YOUNG READERS

NEW YORK

**TO ALL THE YOUNG,
POWERFUL BLACK GIRLS OUT THERE,
YOUR VOICE MATTERS.**

Library of Congress Cataloging-in-Publication Data is available upon request.
ISBN 978-1-9848-5154-3 (trade) — ISBN 978-1-9848-5155-0 (lib. bdg.) —
ISBN 978-1-9848-5156-7 (ebook)

MANUFACTURED IN CHINA
10 9 8 7 6 5 4 3 2 1
First Edition

Contents

1

BECOMING THE "BOOKING QUEEN"

Have you ever asked your parents the story behind your name? When I did, my mom told me some things that really surprised me. When my mom was young, she got sick and her doctor said she might not be able to get pregnant. She was devastated because she wanted children more than anything. After years of praying for a girl, my mom miraculously got pregnant with me. She wanted to celebrate by giving her daughter a special name. A friend had mentioned the name Sky, and my mom loved it! She was a bit of a free bird, and Sky made her think of freedom and possibilities—someone who was able to live life exactly as God created. So one day while she was looking out the window, my mom began to think about how she wanted to spell my name.

Sky, no, Skye. No, there are too many Skyes. I want to do something different. What's another way to spell sky? Hmm . . . what rhymes with sky? Bye, dry, fly, lie, nigh, pie, sly, Thai . . .

That's it! Skai!

The spelling Skai made sense to her. Because already, while I was in her belly, she knew I would be special. Not necessarily a star or celebrity, but an influencer. And it looks like she was right.

♥

Let's start out by agreeing on one thing: babies are cute. Even though they cry and need their diapers changed, their big beautiful eyes and infectious grins can light up a room and make even the most stone-faced person crack a smile. Add in their irresistible laughter, and you have an adorable baby. However, since everyone thinks their baby is pretty, my mom didn't pay a lot of extra attention to people who told her that I

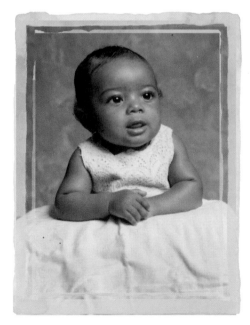

was adorable. I mean, she's from New York. Nothing fazes New Yorkers. Babies are cute. So what? #EverybodyKnowsThat #ButIReally WasCuteEvenIfIDoSaySoMyself

Apparently I never went through a fussy stage. When I was just five months old, my mom remembers people telling her that I was unusually friendly. I wasn't like most babies and toddlers, who are shy and turn their face away from strangers, or try to

hide behind their mother's legs. When my mom would take me out in my stroller every day on a walk around Prospect Park, in Brooklyn, women would constantly talk to me because I was so friendly. Even the people at our favorite neighborhood restaurant thought I had a great personality. It seems like I was just born that way.

My mom spent a lot of time reading *Parents* magazine when I was a baby, and in one issue they ran a column where a mom asked how she could get her child into modeling. At first, my mom thought nothing of it, but when the next issue ran a list of modeling agencies, she was intrigued. My mom's aunt gave her the courage to go for it. She thought maybe I could earn enough money as a model to pay for my college education.

My mom found some pictures she'd had taken of me at JCPenney the previous Christmas and sent them to two modeling agencies. In one set of pictures, I was wearing a fuzzy white jumper with a pink turtleneck, pale-gold shimmery tights, and pink boots with white fur around the top—they looked like little Uggs. In the second photo, I was sitting in a tin tub wearing just my diaper, with a pink-and-blue

towel hanging out of it. Can't you just see it? (I told you I was cute!) There was no way to be certain, of course, but my mom sensed that something amazing was about to happen.

Two weeks later, a famous agency, Wilhelmina Models, called. My mom was super excited and scheduled an in-person meeting with them for the next day. Then, two hours after Wilhelmina called, Generation Models contacted her. They were interested in me too! Having two prestigious modeling agencies want-

ing to represent you isn't something that happens every day. But since she had already set up an appointment with Wilhelmina, my mom decided to work with them. I kicked off my professional modeling career when I was just nine months old.

Now, when a lot of people think of modeling, cool clothes, catwalks, and exotic locations come to mind. But I was too young for much of that, so let me give you a behind-the-scenes peek at how child modeling

actually works. Companies hire modeling agencies to send them talent—that's what they call us actors and models—to help them bring their creative ideas to life. The jobs can range from a print magazine ad or a television commercial to a movie—but that's rare. The agencies then contact the talent who is the best fit for the client's vision. When you're sent on an audition for a modeling job, like being photographed for a magazine article or ad, that meeting is called a go-see. You go to get seen and interviewed for the job. Get it?

My first go-see was with *Parenting* magazine. They needed some baby photographs for an upcoming issue of another publication they owned, *Babytalk*. That's where I came in. Just three days after I was signed by Wilhelmina, I got the gig!

The photo shoot took place one month later. That's when they discovered that not only did I have a very interesting look, but on set I was incredibly easy to work with. The kid wranglers—the adults whose job it is to keep

children safe and occupied until it's time for them to go on set—smiled and helped my mom keep me entertained. Then when I got on set they would call, "Oh, Skai!" and make silly faces. Being the friendly and easygoing baby I was, I would smile, giggle, and laugh as the photographer captured my cutest moments.

Click! Click! Click!

A few months later, my picture appeared next to the magazine's feature story. But you know the really funny thing? When they took my picture, I was all by myself on the set, and when the magazine came out, I was sitting between two other babies. It's amazing what you can do with Photoshop! So that's how my dream career began: sitting on a set with a bunch of grown-ups standing around trying to entertain me. Not a bad life!

I got another photo shoot for *Babytalk* right away. This time I had to sit in a high chair. My picture was used to illustrate an article. Only two months into my modeling career and I'd already worked two jobs. No Paris, Tracy Reese dress, or red-bottom shoes, but hey, I was still wearing a diaper! #MommyPlease-HurryUpAndChangeMe

Right after that, I booked an advertisement for Fisher-Price toys. It wasn't long before I had several go-sees a week.

When I was three, my mom and I shot a cover together for *Parenting* magazine. Oh, wait a minute—I think I left that part out. My mom, did I tell you she's very pretty? Sometimes clients would want to book both of us, but she always said no because she was trying to promote me, not herself. Anyway, for this shoot they dressed us in these really cute pink springtime outfits. When the issue was published, it became one of the highest-selling *Parenting* magazines ever. Because, totally randomly, that month the *Live with Regis and Kelly* TV show was having a contest where parents were invited to submit pictures of their baby in order to win an opportunity to be on the cover. So every day for two weeks, Kelly Ripa held up the issue with us on the front. Back then, it was almost unheard of for anyone Black to be on the cover of a magazine. So in addition to people buying the magazine so they could participate in the promotion, lots of Black mothers bought the issue so they could see a mommy and baby that looked like them. We were part of history, my mom and me. Which, now that I look back on it, is pretty amazing.

By then my mom was starting to understand that it was important for me to have a unique look in order to land these jobs. She also knew that society made lots of Black girls feel bad about their hair, which tends to grow up toward the sun, while many other people's hair grows down toward the earth. Black hair also tends to be very curly. You might have loose curls, tight curls, coils, or a Z pattern. Or it may be frizzy or kinky and not seem to have a pattern at all. No matter the style, unlike straight hair, our curls need to be oiled and given tender loving care.

My mom had grown up feeling embarrassed about her hair, so she put relaxers and other chemicals on it to straighten it. But chemicals can burn your scalp, dry out your hair, and cause it to break off. She didn't want that for me.

Instead, my mom wanted me to feel proud of how God made me. So once I was four years old, she started styling me with natural hair, mostly a two-strand twist. Sometimes she would create just one or two, but other times she'd create them all over my head. Or she would untwist my hair and fluff it up into a twist-out. When she did that, my hair would float out into the air and I would look like the free person she had always imagined I would be.

Around that time Ford Models began to represent me. I got a lot of jobs: Target, Kmart, Ecko Red, The Children's Place, Saks Fifth Avenue. I became one of those famous Gap babies, and I was on the cover of the FAO Schwarz magazine. Eventually the list of jobs I'd booked included just about every company you can think of.

Clients and readers seemed to be drawn to my hair. It turns out that my two-strand twist set me apart from everyone else, especially when we untwisted it and I wore it out. But most hairstylists didn't know what to do with it. They would ask if they could straighten my hair, either with heat or chemicals. But my mom would always tell them no. She had rules that the stylists had to follow: no heat, no hair spray, no water, no wet products—that would damage my hair and ruin my look.

My mom says I got so much work that sometimes the parents of other models were annoyed to see us. "Skai gets all the work," they'd complain to each other. "Our children don't have a chance!" But every time my mom would take me on an audition, the clients would tell her, "We work with a lot of kids, and your daughter is different. We can tell that she is going to be something someday." As a matter of fact, I got so much work, my mom started calling me the Booking Queen. Plus, my clients were all about the twist-out! #NaturalHair

♥

You may be thinking that we were living large and in charge with all the work I was getting, but things at home weren't as easy. While I was giggling and playing in front of the camera, my mom was scrambling behind the scenes. On top of that, most child models don't get paid a lot of money, and what we do get paid has to go into the bank and our parents can't get it out until we're eighteen. Plus, all the go-sees hap-

pened during the day, when my mom was supposed to be at her job. As a single mom, there was an awful lot she had to do by herself. So my mom had to face a tough dilemma. Should she keep working at the post office, knowing that even though her job paid the bills and helped her to save a little money it wasn't where she wanted to be long-term? Or should she take a huge risk and quit so I could have a modeling or acting career and one day go to college and live my dream? More than anything, she wanted me to have opportunities she didn't have. These are the kinds of sacrifices parents make—usually without even telling us! #MomCrushMonday

After saving up some money, my mom resigned from her job so she could focus on my career. By then, I had gone from three go-sees a week to sometimes three a day. Things were definitely looking up! To save money, she moved us out of our apartment and back home with her mom, who lived in a high-rise on Staten Island. But even though my mom had saved, it didn't take long before times started getting tough again. She would usually get another job to save up, and then quit. Over and over, she had to choose between a job and continuing to go on auditions with me. But she never forgot what the agents told her: "Skai is different. Keep going with her . . . don't stop." And so she listened—even if it sometimes meant digging through her pockets for train money.

One day things got so bad that before she read to me at bedtime, she started looking for change between the couch cushions. As I look back, it's really amazing to think that my mom sacrificed so much for me. The good news is, she found enough money for us to take the train. The bad news is, she must have been looking pretty stressed out because the next morning on the train a woman started tapping her on the arm.

"Here, here, take this," the lady said.

My mom thought the woman was going to hand her some kind of flyer. Instead she gave her a twenty-dollar bill.

What?! My mom looked at the woman, puzzled. How did she know that we needed the money?

"Okay, thank you so much," she said. It turns out the woman had given her just enough money to take me to my go-sees the next day. My mom had never seen her before, and she hasn't seen her since. But to this day, just thinking of this moment brings my mom to tears.

That wasn't the only time something like that happened to us. Once, my mom and I were catching the Staten Island Ferry to Manhattan during rush hour, and a homeless man sitting on the ground called out to her. The next thing my mom knew, he was handing her a ten-dollar bill.

"I want you to have it," the man said.

"No, I can't take that!" my mom replied.

"Please take it for you and your daughter."

It was just another incident that my mom took as a sign. "Keep going, don't stop."

♥

By the time I started kindergarten, I had been getting some pretty big breaks.

When I was five years old, I was cast in a Band-Aid commercial that became very popular. The commercial was filmed in New Jersey on a very hot day. A little boy and I ran around a big grassy backyard chasing a fluffy white dog. "I am stuck on Band-Aid brand 'cause Band-Aid's stuck on me!"

On the street, on the bus, on the subway—everywhere, really—it seemed like people were recognizing me.

"Hey, isn't that that girl?"

I just wanted to hide. Although I came alive in front of the camera, I didn't like attention in real life. But it seemed to follow me, even to school. One afternoon in an assembly when I was in the second grade, the administrators were like, "Oh, we have a celebrity who goes to our school!" Then they pointed me out.

Everyone turned and looked at me. I wished I could make myself invisible. Then they wanted me to sing the Band-Aid song. I was so embarrassed! I sang it, but I didn't want to be singled out. It may not surprise you to know that during that time, a couple of girls started picking on me: "You're too short!" "You think you're special."

I didn't realize this would be just the beginning of my experience with bullying.

After the Band-Aid commercial, there was a Kraft cheese ad with me eating a grilled cheese sandwich, and a Yellowbook phone book ad (from back when everyone had landlines and even before Google!). One where a cat crawled out of the Thanksgiving turkey: "That's nasty!" I said. Then there was a politician's TV ad: "What's your position on bedtime?" I asked with my arms crossed like I was a voter he had to convince. There was also a RadioShack gift card ad: "You're the best dad in the world. I'm going to get a pony!"

I was also in this great Target print ad. I remember that one like it was yesterday. I sat on the floor and banged on a lot of pots and pans without a care in the world. It was like, "Okay, this is fun!" Apparently, they wanted to capture my "moments."

Then one day my mom and I were at an audition.

"Oh, I love Skai's billboard," one of the other mothers said.

"What billboard?" my mom asked.

"You didn't know?"

"No!"

So right after I finished that audition, my mom and I got on the subway, walked through the maze of underground tunnels and the hustle and bustle of people, and came out at Times Square—one of the most famous intersections in the world. I'm sure you've seen Times Square on TV. It's filled with so many bright and flashing lights and all sorts of amazing billboards and videos.

That's when my mom pointed way up in the sky and said, "Look!"

There I was, banging on pots on top of a huge red billboard in Times Square. My twist-out and lively eyes had taken over New York.

"Wow!"

Then my mom pulled out her phone and took a picture of it. That is one of my favorite moments, and it was pretty surreal. I still love going to Times Square.

More people started to fall in love with my hair. Some of the other models asked my mom how she did it. And soon I saw more and more little girls on the street wearing natural styles like me.

Still, every now and then a stylist would ask if they could straighten my hair. My mom was like, "Don't even try it!"

A lot of crossover takes place between modeling and acting. So as my modeling career took off, I learned about acting opportunities. I started auditioning for movies and got my first role as a three-year-old girl named Destiny in the movie *Liberty Kid* when I was four. That's when I caught the acting bug and realized I wanted to become an actress.

I began to imagine myself on screen while watching TV. One of the first shows I loved was *That's So Raven* on Disney Channel, starring Raven-Symoné. I was a really big fan of hers—and still am now. Raven got her start as a child model as well, becoming the face of Jell-O, Cool Whip, and other brands. There were hardly any Black actors on TV back then, and Raven-Symoné was a trailblazer. So I was like, okay, she's a young Black girl like me. If she can model and act, I can too. Raven helped me imagine what future opportunities were possible for me.

My mom and I also watched a lot of movies. Even before I started kindergarten, she would often take me to the movie theater on days I wasn't working. She wanted me to watch how different actors performed, because she knew my modeling career could lead to acting. Sometimes we would binge-watch movies at home on Saturdays. I remember this amazing child actor Miko Hughes, who was barely two years old when he performed in *Pet Sematary*. "Mimic him, Skai," my mom would tell me, rewinding the video so we could watch it again.

Having me imitate actors was my mom's way of giving me acting lessons on a budget. Some moms and dads hire acting coaches or send their kids to acting school, but we couldn't afford that.

AnnaSophia Robb was one of my favorite actresses. Since we were close in age, I used to watch her movies all the time, fantasizing about being in her shoes. I loved *Bridge to Terabithia,* which she starred in with Josh Hutcherson. Little did I know that I was about to meet her in real life. When I was four, *Child* magazine held a fashion show during New York Fashion Week, when the fashion industry introduces their new collections. I walked the runway wearing a leopard dress with my hair teased high. (Oh my gosh, they walk so fast, I could hardly keep up!) AnnaSophia Robb walked in it too.

"I want to move to LA and continue acting and modeling," I told my mom.

"Are you sure?" my mom asked me.

"Yes," I told her. "This is something I want to do."

My mom wanted me to explore possibilities by doing what I enjoyed. And she really wanted me to try new things before I said no, which I did sometimes.

"Did you try it?" she'd ask.

"No, I just don't want to."

"Well, I don't think you should say no until you give it a chance."

Even today, this has helped me learn to be open to new experiences.

I was good at drawing and painting, so when I was six my mom signed me up for classes at the School of Visual Arts in New York.

My mom also wanted to expose me to dance. When I was seven, I got a scholarship to the Dance Theatre of Harlem, the world-famous dance and ballet school. My mom used to be a dancer, and she thought I might like it too. For almost two years, I took ballet, jazz, tap, and African dance classes. Jazz and African were my favorite styles.

♥

When I was seven, I guest-starred on two TV shows set in New York: *Royal Pains* and *Rescue Me*. I started getting some voice-over work on *Bubble Guppies* and *Dora the Explorer* on Nickelodeon. I could read my lines the night before and record them the next day. With voice-over work, you can show up in your pajamas and no one will care. I never did that, but I could have.

When I was eight, I got a gig as a "library girl" in the movie *Arthur*, which starred Russell Brand. We filmed very late at night. And Russell Brand, well, he started his entertainment career as a comedian. He's extremely silly in person. He is always saying something hysterical or outrageous. It was hard to say all my lines because you can't help but laugh when you're with him.

In 2009, I appeared in a movie called *The Rebound*, where I played a girl in a museum. And in 2010, I played the role of the Kicking Girl in *The Smurfs*, and I had to kick Neil Patrick Harris. That was kind of hard for me. My mom had always taught me to be very nice and say please and thank you. Now I was supposed to kick him? I'd never done any-

thing like that before. I was so
scared! *Oh my gosh, I'm going to
hurt him!* But thankfully he had
a knee pad on to protect himself.

In March 2011, when I was
eight going on nine, I auditioned for my mom's favorite
TV series, HBO's *Boardwalk
Empire,* and was awarded the
role of Adeline, the daughter
of Chalky White, one of the main characters. When I found out that I
got the part, I was really excited because I had auditioned with a lot of
amazing girls.

Later that month, I went to my agent's office to try out for a role on
the Disney Channel show *Jessie.* Since I had watched Disney Channel
growing up, I thought, "Oh, this will be fun!"

The role was a character named Zuri, who was seven years old. I had
just turned nine, but I was very small for my age. Maybe if my mom
dressed me younger, I could get the part. I had the smarts and maturity
of a nine-year-old but looked like I was seven. My agent recorded me in
the office, then I left.

The opportunity was super exciting, but you never know if you'll get
the part. So I treated it just like any other audition. For both go-sees and
auditions, my mom had taught me to smile, do my best, then continue
about my business and not think about it anymore. Basically, you can't

worry too much about whether you got a job since you can't control it. Lots of times how you auditioned has nothing to do with whether they choose you. They might be looking for someone short and you're tall. Or someone who sings and you don't. You can't get caught up in it. You have to do the best you can and let it go.

Plus, there were others things to be excited about! I filmed my first episode of *Boardwalk Empire,* which was my first experience with a recurring role in a TV series. Up until that point, I had only done guest spots. It took us more than four hours to shoot one scene that was only three pages long. That part of the experience was dreadful. That's when I learned what it takes to shoot a scene with one camera. They had to capture different angles, get a wide shot, a tight shot, the different actors' reactions. But I felt like I was finally on the road to becoming a real actor, where I could develop my character. I was living the dream!

♥

About a month passed between when I auditioned for *Jessie* and when we heard back from Disney. "The Disney people really like Skai and want to fly you guys out to LA tomorrow for a screen test," my manager told my mom. A screen test is when you act on the set in front of a camera so they can decide if you have good chemistry with the other actors and are the best candidate for a role.

Disney! Tomorrow?!

But that's just how things go in this business—you might not hear about anything for weeks, and then it's a rush. It sounded like the break we'd been waiting for, and I'd always wanted to go to LA, so my mom and I had to move fast!

"There's just one catch," our manager told her. "Before she can get on the plane, she has to give up *Boardwalk Empire*."

"Give up *Boardwalk Empire*?!"

"Yes."

"But she just got that! And a screen test doesn't guarantee anything," my mom said. She was right. Being offered a screen test means you pretty much have the job, but if the chemistry's not right, you won't get it. "Why can't she do both?"

"Because *Boardwalk Empire* films on the East Coast and *Jessie* will film in Los Angeles," my manager explained. "Skai can't be in two places at once. She has to choose."

"We still don't know if she's going to get the role!"

"Look, this is just how the process goes," my manager said. "It's a privilege to get to work with Disney. Think it over quickly, then call me back."

My mom and I just sat there looking at each other with our eyes wide and our mouths hanging open.

"Oh my gosh, I can't believe it!" I said, excited about the new possibility.

"But, Skai, you just got *Boardwalk Empire*!"

"But maybe I can have a bigger part on the Disney Channel show!"

"If you had to choose one, what would you want to do?" she asked me.

"I've always wanted to be an actress. I think I should go to LA."

"Are you sure?" my mom asked.

"Yes, Mom, this is my dream."

So my mom called the manager back. "Okay, we'll take it and give up *Boardwalk Empire,*" she said.

Together, we took a gamble. It was a really big move.

♥

The following morning, my mom carefully twisted my hair. She dressed me in denim overall shorts, a turquoise short-sleeved T-shirt, and turquoise Converse sneakers.

Then we flew to Los Angeles. Our flight had a layover in Phoenix. The second plane ride got bumpy, and I started feeling nauseous. When we finally landed and got off the plane, we caught a taxi straight to my audition. I was still feeling motion sickness from the flight.

It was early May, and for the past few weeks, it had been cloudy and rainy, a typical April in New York. But Los Angeles was the exact opposite.

"Oh, wow, the weather's so nice here!" I told my mom. "I've never seen that type of tree before."

"Those are palm trees."

I felt like I was in a dream—I had always imagined myself being in LA. But motion sickness kept bringing me back down to earth.

"Do you have to throw up?" the taxi driver asked. "Just let me know and I can pull over."

"I think she'll be okay," my mom told him.

But now that we were getting close, I started feeling nervous about my screen test. I hoped my queasy stomach would calm down before we got there.

Then, the next thing I knew, the contents of my stomach started bubbling up really fast. At that point, we were on the highway and there was no place to go. My mom reached over to open the window. Too slow!

I vomited all over the window and floor!

Somehow my audition outfit stayed clean.

Fortunately, the taxi driver was really, really nice about it, and by the time we pulled up to the filming studio, my stomach had calmed down.

At the studio in Burbank, we were greeted by writers, producers, and even some executives from Disney. My mom checked my hair to make sure it was neat, then pulled my twists into low pigtails to make me look even younger.

Once they called me into the audition, they asked me to memorize more than ten pages of lines.

"Okay, Skai, we're gonna give you these sides now," they told me. Rather than an entire script, including the parts that your character isn't a part of, they give you sides, just the pages from the script that include your character. "We want you to take them, then come back in ten minutes and we're gonna act it out."

I had never had to learn so many lines before, so my mom and I went over them together, then I went back in the room to audition. To this day, I have no idea how I pulled it off.

After that, they kept putting me through different scenarios. On the inside, I was nervous and shaking. But along the way, I started to get a good feeling about how things were going—they were asking me a lot of questions, and it seemed like they really wanted to get to know me.

"Do you sing?"

"No, I don't sing." (I mean, I have a decent voice, but it's not my thing.)

"Can you do impressions of people?"

I had never done an impression before, but I took a shot at imitating Russell Brand because he was so funny and goofy. I knew they weren't expecting it to be perfect, but they loved it—they couldn't stop laughing!

"Okay, can you go back to your mom and ask her to take your hair down?"

"You mean have her take out my ponytails?"

"Yes, can she do that for us?"

I ran out to the lobby where my mom was waiting. "Mom, Mom, they want you to take my hair out!"

"Okay, okay!" she said, and untwisted my hair. Then she fluffed it up, and it leapt to life all over my head.

When I went running back into the room, they asked me, "Do you know the new song 'Whip My Hair' by Willow Smith?"

"Yes . . ."

"We want you to pretend that you're Willow and sing and act the song out!"

So I started singing and swinging my head around. "I whip my hair back and forth. I whip my hair back and forth."

It was fun—and they loved it!

So did my hair. It did an African dance in the air.

In an instant, my audition was over. The next day we flew back to New York. Los Angeles had been a whirlwind of palm trees and dreams! I couldn't help but wonder: would this be my big break?

HEADING FOR HOLLYWOOD

We got "the call" from Disney on Monday.

My mom had picked me up from school, and we had just walked into our building and taken the elevator to the fourth floor when her phone started ringing.

"All right, are you ready for this?" my manager asked her as she slid the key into the lock of apartment 4H. "Are you sitting down? I've got good news—the Disney people really like Skai, and she booked it."

"Oh my gosh!"

"WHAT, MOM?!"

"Skai, you got it. DISNEY!"

I screamed and jumped up and down!

"When do we have to be there?" my mom asked.

"In two weeks. They want you to stay for six weeks."

"Oh my gosh!" my mom said, laughing while holding my hand and celebrating with me. "The show has been green-lighted for six episodes. When you're there, they'll probably tell you it's going to become a series."

I thought about all the Disney shows I had watched over the years: *That's So Raven, Hannah Montana, Lizzie McGuire* . . . the list was long.

"How about your friends at school? You'll miss them."

By now I had gone to a few different schools. And my mom had always told me I'd make new friends wherever I went. She'd been right.

"I'll just make friends there."

So my mom called the agent back. "We're gonna go to Los Angeles!"

♥

A couple of weeks later, we arrived in LA and checked into an extended-stay hotel.

Right before we started filming, we were invited to a mixer at a restaurant in Hollywood to meet the writers, producers, executives, actors, and other members of our team. I wore a two-strand twist, which my mom set off with a headband.

It turned out one of my costars, Peyton List, was from New York. We'd modeled together a handful of times, beginning back when I was four and Peyton was eight. So it was good to see a familiar face. Karan

Brar had played Chirag Gupta in the *Diary of a Wimpy Kid* movie. I'd loved *Wimpy Kid* . . . it was so funny!

I also met Cameron Boyce. He'd been in a movie called *Grown Ups* starring Adam Sandler, which was one of my favorites. Oh my gosh, I couldn't believe I would be on the same show with these people!

Of course, we were really wowed that the star of the show would be Debby Ryan! We all knew her from when she had been on *Barney & Friends* and *The Suite Life on Deck* on Disney when she was younger.

Debby would play the star of the show, Jessie, an eighteen-year-old girl with big dreams, who rebels against her father by leaving the military base she lives on in Texas to go to the Big Apple, where she becomes the nanny for the Ross family and moves into their multimillion-dollar penthouse apartment.

The Rosses are super-rich jet-setters who are away a lot. They have four kids: Luke, Emma, Ravi, and Zuri. Our diversity was an important part of the show. Peyton would play Emma, the Rosses' only biological kid. Emma was white, seventeen years old, and into fashion and shopping. Luke, Ravi, and Zuri were adopted. Luke was biracial and originally

from Detroit. He was athletic but not very smart. Ravi was smart but not very athletic. He was adopted from India. I would play Zuri, the youngest sibling, who was adopted from Uganda. When we started out, Zuri was just seven. She was very independent, empowered, and knew what she wanted. And she would be an important part of the story line from the very first episode!

We learned that we would be filming at a place called Hollywood Center Studios, not the official Disney lot. A number of famous old TV shows had been filmed there, from *I Love Lucy* to *The Fresh Prince of Bel-Air,* which starred Willow Smith's dad, Will Smith, to *Wizards of Waverly Place,* starring Selena Gomez. Movies were filmed there too: *Karate Kid, Bad Santa, Dumb and Dumber.* Many amazing actors became legends there.

LIGHTS, CAMERA, ACTION!

I will always remember my first day of work! It was early June, and the sky in LA was all hope and possibilities. I couldn't believe it when we pulled up to the studio gates and saw the Hollywood Studios sign.

"Oh my gosh, Mom, this is my dream!"

"Skai, I am so proud of you," my mom told me. "You've worked hard for this!"

We pulled through the big white gates and checked in at the security booth, and the guard waved us through.

"You're all the way to the back on the right."

So we drove through the center of the lot. There were a bunch of windowless, pink, two- and three-story, industrial-looking buildings on each side. Nothing special. As we drove through the complex, it was like we were moving in slow motion. My eyes were so wide and my mouth just hung open. I was living in a fantasy!

Then we pulled up to the set: Stage 3/8. It was huge! A young woman was waiting out front for us.

"Welcome to Hollywood Center Studios," she said with a cheery voice as she reached out her hand. "I'm Lori Carter, one of the production coordinators. I'll be getting you oriented." Then she typed in a security code and let us into the building. "We are so excited to have you here. First, let me show you to your dressing room."

A dressing room! Was this really happening? I wanted to pinch myself!

As she led us back to my dressing room, she pointed out other offices. On the left was the AD, or assistant director's, office. The ADs make sure the right people are on set at the appropriate time and keep things running smoothly overall.

The dressing rooms were on the other side of the hall. Suddenly I found myself standing in front of a door with a plaque that read: *Skai Jackson, Jessie.*

"Skai, this will be your dressing room," Lori said, pushing open the door to the place where I'd spend most of my time over the next four years. The room was super simple. The walls were white, and there were two basic couches and a table in it. A welcome basket sat on the table with little Disney trinkets in it: a cup, a blanket, a plastic bear, and a thank-you note.

"Wow, I have my own room!" I said. My dreams were coming true!

"It has potential," my mom said. I could almost see the gears in her head turning. Within a few days, she would get bright pink decorative pillows for my couches, a pink paper lamp, a cute bright pink bean bag chair that I could lie on, a little chest to store all my knickknacks, and pink and red daisies growing up my walls. My mom has an eye for design.

Next, Lori showed us craft services, which is what people call the place where food, refreshments, and many other supplies are available all day for the entire cast and crew.

Then she took us upstairs. That's where we'd do all our fittings, wardrobe, and hair and makeup. That's also where we'd take our classes. Yep, even though I was a Hollywood actress, I still had to go to school.

After that, she took us downstairs and out to the stage.

I'd always imagined that the stage of a TV set would have its own special, long hall leading to it and that the walls would be black and the stage-door red with gold writing on it. This one had just a generic black door marked *Stage* in white writing. But I never will forget the first time I opened that door. I was like, "Wow!" as I slowly walked through it, wide-eyed with amazement!

There was a living room with a gray sofa, blue chairs, a fireplace, and a blue-carpeted staircase with gold banisters that went to the second floor. Floor-to-ceiling windows provided a view of the neighboring skyscrapers and the trees of Central Park. Being on the set was almost like I was home. I wanted to sidestep the yellow taxis flying down Broadway, wind my way through people lined up at the newsstands, and race down the steps to catch the subway.

It was just freakin' awesome!

Then I walked out of the living room through the doors into the kitchen. The floors were black-and-white tile, the walls were lavender, and there was a big wooden table where the whole family could sit. I could almost smell cookies baking.

Then there was my bedroom. Oh my gosh, it was so pretty. There were pink carpet and curtains, and light blue and green walls with flower paintings on them—the kind of bedroom any girl would die for! Even better than the one my mom had created for me back in our apartment in Harlem.

There were sets for the subway, Central Park, different bedrooms. Everything was better than I could ever have imagined. I jumped around with excitement. I couldn't believe that this would be my new life!

♥

But I was about to learn that acting could be very challenging.

Up until that point, I had only done commercials and onetime appearances in movies. I'd filmed a single episode of *Boardwalk Empire,* my first television show. I would discover that filming a TV series was really, really different—there was just so much to do!

Okay, so here's how a typical day would go: I would wake up at six in the morning to get to work by eight. When I would arrive on set, I would go straight to school and there were teachers there to help me. Most days we had four hours of school, but on Thursday and Friday, which were our shooting days, we had three hours of school. On our weeks off from shooting, we would get in extra hours of school to make up for the short days. I'll tell you more about how that worked later.

After school we would rehearse, and after rehearsal we would do fittings. We would have fittings on Mondays and Tuesdays. Our stylists, Bridget and Mary-Kate, and a team of three assistants helped create the look for my character.

On the days we filmed, I would also go to hair and makeup. I would go to wardrobe first so I wouldn't have to worry about messing up my hair while I was pulling my outfit over my head. I knew my hairstyle would require extra care, and I didn't want it getting messed up. In the beginning I had a Black stylist who had dreadlocks and understood both relaxed and natural Black hair. But it wasn't long before she left to go work on a film.

My natural Black hair is a lot to manage and is different from the rest of the cast's hair, so it requires different skills, especially since it gets damaged easily from heat and styling. My mom is an expert on styling my hair, so she knew that twisting and covering it with a scarf on rehearsal days would make it camera-ready for filming days.

Filming those first six episodes was a lot. There were so many things to learn. And I was the youngest and least experienced member of the cast. The older kids picked things up so quickly—I had to get up to speed fast!

The first thing I had to master was the production schedule. We would get our script on Friday. Then on the weekend, I took it upon myself to study my lines so I would be extra prepared for each week's show. On Monday, Tuesday, and Wednesday, we would rehearse together.

Okay, let's start with Monday. We would go into the studio for a table read. That's where all the actors, writers, and producers sit around a large table in a big meeting room, while the actors read their lines and the writers listen and give notes on how we're reading them.

"Can you say that part faster?"

"Will you change this word to that?"

"I'd like you to read that with more expression. And can you give us a little attitude?"

Sometimes the table reading was hard. I would find my eyes skipping lines.

After the table reading with the writers, we'd practice our new lines a bit. Then we'd have another table read for all the executives and producers. Sometimes they would want us to change things too. We would take notes and practice that version. Oh my gosh, it was demanding! Not only memorizing lines, but also delivering them the way they want you to or the way you think you should do them. But learning was also fun. I was excited to gain so much experience!

On Tuesday and Wednesday, we would run through the scenes. We'd act the scenes out onstage and in the proper set—like the kitchen, my bedroom, or the living room. Disney Channel has multi-camera sets, and I had to learn how to work on one. Rather than just one camera, there were four cameras that I always had to be thinking about.

The director would give us our blocking. Blocking tells us how to move around on the set—where to stand, which way to face, what lighting to stand under, which camera to look at to give the studio audience and viewers the best angle.

"Okay, move this way, cross this way, do this, sit down here."

Having to remember so many different things could be really confusing. I had never realized that you had to think about so much while you were saying your lines. We practiced over and over and over.

I had to learn where to stand to "cheat out" to the cameras. Cheating out basically means, if I need to talk to Ravi over here, but the camera that's filming me is over there, I have to make sure it can see my full face while I'm talking. So not only do I have to walk to the right place and turn my face and body the right way, I also have to look toward but not directly at the camera that's filming me. In fact, I can't look at any of the cameras, even though one of them might be in my face.

Sometimes things could get complicated. There were times where there was so much going on that we would get lost and have to improvise. During really intense scenes where we were all running around or playing tag, we would get so mixed up it would be funny. The great thing was our producers never got mad at us.

With four cameras, the blocking is like choreography. Every one of the actors has to be in the right place at the right time to deliver their lines, and they need to move around very precisely. "Okay, go here, look this way while you say it, and have this facial expression." They might make changes up to the very last minute before we film.

So on Monday, Tuesday, and Wednesday, we would do table readings and rehearse. Then on Thursday and Friday, we would film. Our call times would vary. Sometimes we had to be there at 8, and sometimes it could be 12 or 1—it depended on what scenes we were in that week.

There was a lot of attention on me from the very first episode, because after coming to New York, Jessie runs out of money and gets kicked out of her cab. The building's doorman, Toni, and my character, Zuri, discover Jessie on the sidewalk, and I end up inviting her to be the Ross family nanny.

Everything was really fun, and everyone was happy with my work, and episode one was a wrap!

"All right, moving on. You can go change," the assistant director would tell us when we'd successfully completed a scene.

♥

I thought learning my lines, blocking, and cheating out were hard, until I also found out I had a New York accent. New Yorkers don't even say New York—we say New Yawk. But since everybody around us has an accent, we don't even hear it.

No one corrected the way I talked when I was acting in New York. But my accent affected some of the words I said and made them sound a little different. The dialogue coach helped me out a lot on set so I could get used to saying certain words properly.

"It's not *axe*, it's *ask*," they'd tell me.

"Axe?" I'd ask.

"No, *ask*, Skai," they'd say. "Try it again."

I didn't always understand what they were talking about. It all seemed really weird to me. Sometimes my dialogue coach would come to my dressing room. I'd go over my lines with her, and she'd listen to how I said things. Not *heah*, but *here*. Not *pretsel*, but *pretzel*. I say *aunt*, but the executive director, Pam, wanted me to pronounce it *ant*. My grandfather is from Honduras. In Spanish, he calls plantains *plátanos*. The English pronunciation that he uses for the word plantains is *plan-tans*, but Pam wanted *plan-tanes*. I also had to learn how to pronounce certain sounds, like *ta* or *ka*, more clearly. The training was very structured. I wasn't the only one; everyone in the cast learned to enunciate our words. We would practice our lines over and over until we got them right.

There were so many things I had to worry about. But in spite of all that, I loved it!

"We're done, we're wrapped! See you next week!"

After four episodes, we got the official word. They told us that when the first six episodes were done, we would get a five-week break, then come back to film seven more episodes, for a total of thirteen.

My mom started looking for a place for us to live. LA is a very expensive city. The week after we finished filming, she finally found an apartment in this cute little town called Studio City. So we headed back to New York to pack up our stuff and officially move across the country. We had four weeks to handle everything at home and move to LA.

When we got back to New York, even though I loved it, everything suddenly seemed different. Whenever we rode the subway, I felt a little tense—there was just too much going on, too many people. I hadn't realized it at the time, but the slower pace of LA life had started to grow on me. I liked seeing palm trees and blue sky. Even being stuck in LA rush-hour traffic seemed better than speeding around underground on the subway. At least I had more privacy and people weren't always recognizing me. I didn't miss bumping into people, the sound of horns honking, always walking so fast, or having to be aware of my surroundings.

In the meantime, my mom had to sell most of our stuff. After the apartment was cleared out, the moving trucks were gone, and everything was squared away, I could tell that she felt like she could relax.

The next morning, we went to JFK Airport to catch our flight to Burbank. As good as the city had been to me, New York was a wrap.

Now it was time to move on. I was an official Hollywood actress! Disney had bought us seats in first class. It was our very first time! We took a selfie to mark the occasion.

I sat in the window seat and admired the view as our plane took off. The amazing New York City skyline, the Empire State Building, the Chrysler Building, the Brooklyn Bridge—I could see them all. My mom even pointed out the Statue of Liberty, which had invited so many people to come to America and start a new life. I was grateful to the city that sent me shooting like a star into my dreams. As we climbed through the clouds, I realized the sky was the limit.

Late that August, I reported to Hollywood Center Studios to start filming the rest of *Jessie*'s first season. I felt inspired and awestruck. Not only was this a super opportunity, but I'd learned that our exact set had once been the set of *That's So Raven*. I took that as a sign of good luck. Maybe one day I would become as popular as Raven was!

Even though I arrived on the set ready to work, with a better understanding of what to expect, I still couldn't even believe this was happening to me.

♥

So, if you haven't been able to tell, even though acting feels like playing to me, it was very hard work.

For one thing, we had to do a lot of fittings for my wardrobe. In the beginning, Disney's vision was that they wanted me to wear tutus and leggings. That just wasn't really my style, even when I was much younger. I usually wore jeans and a cute shirt, but I was playing a role and had to dress like someone else. I wore tutus and leggings for two seasons. It wasn't until season three that my character started wearing fewer tutus. I was so stoked when they finally let my character's style evolve and I wasn't dressed in those kinds of outfits anymore.

As far as the script, one day it would be fine, then the next day they might change ten of my lines. I'd have to learn them all over again. As I got older and more experienced, sometimes they changed even more of the script. It could be a lot to learn, and occasionally I would get flustered. I was so worried I wouldn't be able to remember all my new lines. To this day, people ask me how I memorized so much. Honestly, I don't know how I did it. Rehearsing a lot really helped.

At times a cast member would tell a funny joke and we would get the giggles. We would start laughing and just couldn't stop. "Okay, you guys, we need to shoot," they'd tell us. But it could take thirty minutes before we could keep a straight face.

About once a week, we filmed in front of a studio audience of about a hundred people, sitting in bleachers. It was a lot of fun and it gave us so much energy. On those nights, if we wanted to, we could stay and meet the fans, which I always liked to do! But since there were so many, we might not leave until nine or ten. I learned to always stand in the front of the line so I could keep it moving and go home.

The work could be very tiring, and not every day was perfect, but I really loved what I was doing. Because the scenery and location were so new to me, that whole first year in LA felt like I was living in one big fantasy. When we had time, we would go to the beach like we were on vacation and do all these activities that you can't do in New York.

Jessie premiered on September 30, 2011. We had been taping that day, and they wanted everyone to stay. We watched the first episode on the monitors right there on set. On that very same night, Jaden and Willow Smith visited the set. They had come to the lot to see their friend Mateo Arias, a star of the Disney series *Kickin' It*. Afterward they visited us. WOW!

Later we learned that more than four million people viewed our very first episode!

It wasn't long before the show started becoming very popular. Our ratings were really high. In fact, our ninth episode, "Star Wars," attracted a whopping 7.3 million viewers. People started recognizing me on the street.

"Hey, isn't that Zuri?"

"Zuri, Zuri!"

I was shocked that people wanted to take their picture with me. It would happen at the mall, when I was at the American Girl store getting outfits for my doll. It would happen at restaurants, when I was eating dinner with my mom.

I found being called Zuri to be kind of confusing. Zuri was just a character on TV. I'm Skai. It was really weird, and because I was only nine, it took me a long time to comprehend it.

As a cast, we started going to meet-and-greets, where you "meet" your fans. "Luke, Jessie, Ravi, Emma, Zuri!" That's when I really started to discover how many people were into us. And I hadn't realized the numbers of fans who would want to come out just to see me.

We traveled all around the country. Sometimes our meet-and-greets would be more than three hours long and one thousand, two thousand, three thousand kids would show up and wait for hours. They'd be really excited to get to talk to us. I'd sign a picture and take a group picture with them. Then the next person would come up. It was so much fun—and hectic!

In these conversations and in random encounters on the street,

Black girls started to tell me, "You're such a role model for me" or "I love your hair!" It didn't take long until I started getting mail. My mom and I would read through my fan letters.

"Seeing you makes me think that I can do it."

"You give me hope."

"I wish I could get my hair like that."

My mom got a lot of compliments too:

"Your daughter is such an inspiration."

"You're doing such a great job."

Reading comments like these was rewarding. I had never imagined that girls would look up to me. I began to realize that I was a role model for my fans. But I also knew that Black girls held a special place in their heart for me and I meant something special to them. I knew that it was very important for me to just be myself.

LOOKING BACK IN TIME

In spite of our fame, it didn't take me long to learn that between seasons, the goal for most Disney actors was to book a job outside of Disney. Disney had played a tremendous role in getting my name out there and helping me become so popular, but I wanted to do all sorts of acting in my career—drama, horror, thrillers, all of it. Not just comedy. Between *Jessie*'s first and second seasons, I started auditioning for other roles, and I booked a small part in the movie *G.I. Joe: Retaliation*.

That same year, I got a role in the movie *The Watsons Go to Birmingham*. It was a really important film to me. The movie was about a Black family who lived in Michigan in the 1960s and went to Birmingham, Alabama, for the summer. The Watsons had two boys and a girl. I played their eight-year-old daughter, Joetta. I don't want to spoil the plot for you, but let's just say that the kids weren't ready for life in the South during that time. They also got caught up in a very tragic and unforgettable event in history.

The movie was my first time acting in a film from a whole different era. Even the costumes: long full skirts and bobby socks and saddle shoes. Wow, people wore this stuff? Learning more about discrimination, our nation's history, the clothes—all of it was eye-opening to me.

We filmed in Atlanta for over a month. I got to work with great actors like Anika Noni Rose, David Alan Grier, Wood Harris, and LaTanya Richardson, so I kept a close eye on their acting techniques.

Before we started filming, I read the book, by Christopher Paul Curtis. I was so excited because my homeschool teacher told me, "Everyone in the school has to read the book and is going to have to watch the movie." A lot of my friends saw it. I think all of us learned something about the Civil Rights movement that we didn't know before.

Another cool thing was the author signed my book. I was really grateful for the part. And when my mom thanked the director, Kenny Leon, for selecting me, he told her, "You don't have to thank me. During the audition, she handled everything I threw at her." Since I sometimes wondered if I had grown as an actor, that made me feel good.

The next year I got the part of Lacey Casey in *My Dad's a Soccer Mom,* with Lester Speight and Wendy Raquel Robinson. Lester played a famous football player who got cut from his team and became a soccer

"mom" instead. I was his daughter who played soccer, which is really ironic because I don't play any sports.

So now I had two movies under my belt. That felt like a big deal.

SOME BIG FIRSTS

Since *Wizards of Waverly Place* used to be filmed on our stage, Selena Gomez knew some of our crew. During season two, when Justin Bieber appeared on her show, she brought him to visit our set. It was such a big surprise!

OH MY GOSH!

Of course, it happened on the one day that my mom had left early. I called her from a producer's office.

"Hello?" she said, sounding strange because she didn't recognize the number.

"Mom," I whispered.

"Skai?!"

"Justin Bieber is here," I said quietly.

"Who?"

"Justin Bieber."

"Ahh!"

"I gotta go, I gotta go!" I said.

Justin stayed to watch us rehearse, and he even took pictures with us. Later, when I went back to my dressing room, he had written a little note on the back of a small poster.

Skai, Nice to meet you! You are very cute, make sure to always stay sweet!! God Bless

During season three, we got the word that the First Lady, Mrs. Michelle Obama, wanted to guest-star on *Jessie*. Apparently one of her daughters was a big fan. The week leading up to the show was intense. The Secret Service went through the entire building. They had to check our dressing rooms. On the day that we filmed, there were like ten cars full of Secret Service. We had to go through metal detectors. There were police in cars. There were snipers on the roof. The whole building was on lockdown.

Mrs. Obama was very sweet. We got to talk a little bit as we did our lines. She asked a lot of questions when she was memorizing them. It was such an honor that she even wanted to come on the show. Shortly after she guest-starred, we were invited to the White House for the Easter Egg Roll. It was a whole-day event, and it was extremely entertaining. There were a lot of different celebrities: Ariana Grande, Big Sean, Jim Carrey, and a whole bunch of others. The White House and the White House lawn are so big, plus they had musical performances. You hear about the famous people there, but you may not get to see them. One year, Beyoncé and Jay-Z were there just walking around and my friend Marsai Martin, who plays Diane Johnson on *Black-ish,* took a picture of them.

We didn't participate in the egg roll, but we did go into the White House. We saw most of the rooms. Then they had us wait in line so we could go into a room where President Barack Obama and the First Lady were standing.

"Oh, hi!" I said to her when my mom and I went in.

"Oh yeah!" she said excitedly. "Barack, this is Skai. Remember? I guest-starred on her show."

The president was very sweet, and even though he was the most powerful man in the world, he was also one of the nicest people I've ever met. We took a picture with them, then we left and participated in some of the activities. It was one of the most exciting moments of my life. President and Mrs. Obama are such an inspiration to me. They help me believe that everything is possible and that I should always reach for the sky. And to think it happened all because of our show!

LIVING THE DREAM

Every TV actor has favorite episodes. One of mine was a Halloween show. I was a race-car driver, Emma was a gypsy, and Jessie was a killer nanny. There's a scene where Jessie was running in the lobby, chasing all four of us kids. I wasn't paying attention when I was running and I almost knocked myself out on a corner of the wall. It really hurt! They even had to stop filming—it was so bad, I needed to go to the hospital. I had a big goose egg on my head.

My hardest episode was one when we all pretended to swap bodies and we played each other's roles. I had to play Jessie.

"How in the heck am I going to act like a twenty-year-old?" I wondered.

"Oh, you can do it, Skai! It's gonna be fun!" the producers told me.

"I'm the youngest—I don't know how to act twenty-one!"

We filmed four seasons of *Jessie*. The show became so popular that we ended up on air in Canada, Australia, New Zealand, Ireland, the United Kingdom, Singapore, and South Africa. We averaged more than four million viewers each season.

Along the way, my cast mates were like my brothers and sisters. Peyton and I were especially close. Most of the time we kids got along well. Every now and then, we would fight, just like siblings do. Karan and Cameron were like brothers. Me and Karan? Well, we would get on each other's nerves and butt heads from time to time. Sometimes

it appeared like he didn't like the fact that I was the youngest and got so much attention. He was three years older than me. Everything kind of became a competition. But we got past it and formed a friendship. I mean, you can't get too upset about it—we were all really young.

Overall, filming *Jessie* was one of the most enjoyable experiences I have ever had! Even with the tough days, I really appreciated the opportunity. Because of *Jessie,* I became well known as a comedic actor. After years of scraping and struggling, finally my mom and I were financially

secure. I was getting regular invitations to industry events and friended and shouted out on social media. After years of work, I had arrived. I was really, really proud of myself.

But by season four, I was starting to get tired. Every single weekday, I woke up at six in the morning to be on set by eight for our daily routine. We usually worked until four or five, but some days were longer. I'd never had a real job before, but I know people were counting on me and I needed to show up and do my best.

Finally, after 98 episodes, *Jessie* was a wrap.

During the four years I was on the show, I had accomplished what I wanted to do. I'd followed in the footsteps of the actor I looked up to so much, Raven-Symoné. I'd become really popular among kids my age. And I was excited that other brown girls had started to look up to me just like I had looked up to Raven. I knew I was giving them hope, especially with my natural hair. That inspired me, even though it also came with a lot of responsibility.

All in all, *Jessie* provided me the opportunity to start living the life of my dreams. I'll always be grateful for that chance.

MY NAME'S NOT ZURI!

"Zuri, Zuri! Oh my gosh, it's Zuri!"

I was standing in the makeup aisle at a drugstore looking at the baby-blue nail polish when I heard a bunch of girls calling out the name Zuri.

"Oh my gosh, you're my favorite actress," one girl told me as she ran down the aisle and stood right next to me. "Can I have your autograph?"

"Can we take a selfie with you?" asked her friend.

The girls were jumping up and down, pulling out their phones, extremely excited. My mom was in the car waiting for me. What should I do?

"Uh, okay . . ."

Another time it happened, my mom and I were in the waiting area at the airport. "Oh my gosh, Zuri! Aren't you Zuri from *Jesse*?" We had tried to sit quietly in the corner, but now a grown woman was rushing toward me. It felt a lot like a zombie apocalypse.

"Oh my gosh, you are so cute! My daughter loves you," she said.

"I'm Skai," I said.

Then the woman reached out and grabbed my mother's hand and started shaking it. "Are you her mom?"

"Yes, I'm Skai's mom," she said very formally.

In the beginning, my mom and I didn't always know how to deal with it. I mean, she grew up in New York. She has street smarts. But these were my fans. And she'd taught me to be polite. I didn't want to do anything to offend anyone.

"Oh my gosh, you're doing such a good job with her," the woman continued. "She's my daughter's favorite actress."

"Thank you so much. That's nice," my mom said.

"Can I take a picture for my daughter?"

I looked at my mom. She had a sheepish look on her face.

"Okay . . ."

I didn't want the woman to take my picture, but I didn't want to seem rude, so I said, "Uh, okay . . ."

Then the woman sat down in the empty seat next to me, put her arm around me, and brought her face close to mine to take a selfie. As soon as she left, I scrunched up my face. It was bad enough that she'd called me Zuri and my name is Skai. She had gotten too close, she had on too much perfume, and why did a grown person want a picture with me?

♥

The more popular the show got, the more popular all of us kids got. I had a lot of fun at meet-and-greets, when I knew what was expected of me and my cast mates and the crowd was under control. But fame wasn't always so fun when people I didn't know came up to me in public, especially when I was so little.

When I started getting recognized in public, the situation was really weird for me. I didn't understand what was going on.

I'd go to the mall. "Zuri, Zuri!"

Sometimes at the grocery story. "Excuse me, aren't you Zuri?"

"I'm Skai," I'd try to interject.

"Zuri, that's my daughter over there, and she wants to know if she can take a picture with you."

I never knew what to say. If I said no, I was being ungrateful. If I said yes, it was awkward.

Every now and then I'd see kids standing behind a pole at the mall, trying to take pictures of me secretly. Or I'd see a phone over the top of a menu. That was really overwhelming.

At first, there would be times when I would put my head down or turn my head, hoping they wouldn't see me. I didn't intend to be mean—it was just really uncomfortable and sometimes even scary to me.

My mom often said I should try to understand the situation from the other person's perspective. She would tell me to consider how it must be for the Jonas Brothers or Justin Bieber. I loved my fans and really appreciated that they liked me so much and felt inspired by me, so I tried my best.

But then even more weird situations would happen, and my mom didn't know how to handle it either.

Sometimes adults would want to take a picture with me—that seemed a little strange.

Or I'd be sitting in a restaurant eating dinner with my mom or walking through the mall and hear a mom tell her daughter to go take a picture with me. Lots of times the kid hadn't even known I was there—it was the mom who had seen me.

"Don't you try to handle it, Skai," my mom would say. "Let me be the bad guy when we have to tell them no."

At times the moms could be really aggressive. "Well, this is the life she signed up for."

No, I had signed up to be an actor and work in my passion and craft. I hadn't known all of this would come with it. Plus, I was just a kid!

Then there were times when I would think I had gone into the bathroom by myself. But next thing I knew, somebody or sometimes a lot of people would be standing outside my stall door. When I came out, there was nowhere to hide.

"Can I take a picture with you?"

At first, I was like, "Uh, sure . . ."

Eventually my mom stopped letting me go to the bathroom alone.

My mom and I would often go to CityWalk at Universal Studios near our apartment to shop or to a restaurant or the movie theater just to hang out. Kids would come up to me and ask me to take a picture with them. One time a bunch of kids surrounded me, and security had to escort us back to our car. There was so much running and pushing going on that I ended up feeling a little scared!

Even today, I really like meeting my fans, and I appreciate them for being fans of my work and following me on social media. I almost never say no to getting my picture taken, but truthfully I don't feel comfortable.

♥

As if the sometimes overwhelming interactions with fans weren't enough, whenever I talked to people, they would assume that my personality was like Zuri's. Zuri is very outspoken, has a lot of energy, and does things I wouldn't ordinarily do. Me? I'm kind of shy—I'm a homebody, and I don't talk much.

"You're so different from how you are on TV," they'd say, as though I'd disappointed them.

Other people would say, "You're really chill and laid-back."

Even adults didn't seem to understand that they were watching me play a character. Zuri was not my real personality. I thought it was obvious, but maybe it wasn't. They would tell me they watched the show religiously. But they didn't know the real me.

The public also seems to forget that I'm not nine years old anymore. Even though I'm now sixteen, some fans still treat me like I am a little kid. It can get a little frustrating.

♥

While I didn't always like meeting people in public, social media was a different story.

When *Jessie* first came out, we were all encouraged to be on social media. But my mom didn't think I was ready for it at first because I was so young. I didn't get my Twitter account until I was ten. My mom and I worked together to decide what to post, but she had to approve everything and monitor any fan interactions to keep me safe. No one on the cast had to be on social media, but Disney loved it when we interacted with our fans to make them feel more connected to the show. Every time there was a new episode, we would get photos to post to give our fans a sneak peek.

All cast members and their parents on all Disney Channel shows were given what they called Media Training 101. They explained what we should and should not post, asked us to avoid bad language, and warned us to be careful because posts would be out there forever. Even if you wanted to take back something you posted, by the time you deleted it, fans would already have taken screenshots. This was all great advice.

I liked that I could do that at home—no crowds, no cameras, no creepy adults. I really enjoyed interacting with fans on Twitter and later Instagram, posting pictures and having a lot of followers. It was really exciting. By the time I was ten, I had a million Twitter followers. That was really awesome! The show encouraged us to stay engaged with them. The downside of Twitter was that it came with a lot of trolls and people who say horrible things. I'll tell you all about them later.

When I was either ten or eleven, I also got an Instagram account. My mom had the passwords to my accounts. Since Disney wanted us to build up our followers, I started watching what other kids were doing who had a lot of them—usually kids with like three million or even ten million followers. Zendaya was one person I really looked up to.

By the time I was twelve, lots of kids had started using Vine, so I got a Vine account too. I didn't tell my mom. I figured out that everyone was picking up followers by making silly videos, dancing weird, telling stupid jokes, that kind of stuff. I thought if they did it, I should do it too. Why not?

Sometimes when my mom would take a nap or run an errand, I

would put on silly wigs, act out different personalities, just be silly. I gained a million followers, then two million. It all happened really fast—pretty much right as a lot of people were learning who I was. Back then, they had these things called loops that showed how many times your video got watched. One of my videos had over 25 million loops on it. It also helped me get more Instagram followers.

Even though I had gotten social media training, I was just a kid. I didn't understand the consequences of some of the things they were telling me. It never occurred to me that anything bad could happen.

I remember one day when my mom had run up the street to the supermarket and I was cleaning out my drawers and found this pair of green shorts with oranges and grapefruits on them. I put them on and started silly dancing to the catchy song that I had downloaded to my phone and made a goofy Vine out of it. Little did I know that the gossip columnist Perez Hilton, who is an adult, had been following me. He reposted my video as part of a blog post where he wrote about how inappropriate it was that I was dancing to a song with suggestive lyrics. Suggestive lyrics! What was he talking about? The song was "Anaconda" by Nicki Minaj. I didn't even know what she was singing about. I got a lot of backlash.

"How dare your mom let you listen to that kind of music!"

"Where are your parents?"

My mom discovered what I'd done when she received a Google Alert. That's also how she learned that I had a Vine account. Needless to say, she was very upset. She flipped out and started yelling. "What the heck is this?!" She was really worried that Disney would be upset and it would ruin my career.

Fortunately, when they reached out to her, they told her that they'd been through worse and that it would blow over soon.

I was punished for like two weeks. I couldn't use my phone or watch TV. My mom gave me a lot of lectures.

"First of all, it's dangerous because people can figure out where we live," she told me. I hadn't understood that I needed to be careful about what was in the background when I posted.

"To our family you are a regular kid, but to the outside world you're a star who they look up to. You didn't realize it, but that song is inappropriate. That's why I don't allow you to listen to that kind of music."

It's really embarrassing, but some of these videos still circulate. Even though I did them like eight years ago, every now and then someone will post one as a joke and it will get like 2,000 retweets. They've literally come back to haunt me. I wish I could say it isn't me, but it was. It wasn't my finest hour. Then again, I was only about ten or twelve years old, and I didn't know they would be used against me.

SKAI'S
SOCIAL MEDIA TIPS

If you are using social media or are looking forward to being old enough to use it, I don't want you to experience the pain I went through. So please take it from me:

- Remember, everything you post will be out there forever, so don't do anything crazy.

- If you want to keep your posts for just your friends and family to see, protect yourself by making your page private.

- If someone is being hateful or disrespectful, use the block button. I do.

- Have your parent monitor your account to make sure everything is safe. My mom still monitors mine and has all my passwords.

- When you do fun things and go to exciting places, always document it with a good-quality picture. Find great lighting and take a cute selfie. Make sure you get some pictures to represent you. Social media has its good side too!

♥

Another really difficult thing when you're famous is that you're always getting hacked. Both my Twitter and Instagram have been hacked more than once.

The first time it happened, I had been following a lot of famous people on Twitter, like President Obama, major directors, Justin Bieber, and even my cast mates. Next thing I knew, someone took over my page and started tweeting disgusting, horrible, gross things at all sorts of A-list celebrities. At first, some people thought it was me doing it. I would see them and they would have an attitude with me or they wouldn't talk to me and I wouldn't know why.

One day I was the number one hashtag. The hashtag was even reported about on a major television network. It got so bad that Disney contacted my mom to make sure she was aware of it. They were like, "We know this is not Skai."

So Twitter shut down my account, and I lost all my followers.

My Instagram got hacked around the same time. The person would post at night while I was asleep. I would find out from looking at the comments by my followers in the morning when I woke up. By then the post had been out there for hours and the damage had been done.

It took me a while to get verified on Twitter, which makes it harder for people to impersonate me. But I still haven't gotten all my followers back on either Twitter or Instagram.

♥

After a couple of years, I started to get the hang of being famous. I liked that I could put a smile on a kid's face.

Once I began to feel more comfortable meeting my fans, I would go to more meet-and-greets and take pictures with them. I started to really appreciate them, especially since they watched my TV shows and went to my movies. Now meet-and-greets are one of my favorite parts of my work.

But having fans isn't the only good thing about being famous. You also get free stuff sometimes, like clothes, food, and nail polish. "Wow, okay, I don't have to pay for that? That's cool!"

I've also been invited to events like BET's Black Girls Rock Awards, which encourage girls of color to participate in the arts and challenge the ways we're portrayed in the media; *Vanity Fair*'s Young Hollywood event, the party the magazine hosts the night before the Oscars; and *W Magazine*'s It Girl Luncheon, sponsored by Dior.

You also get to meet some amazing people. In addition to President Obama and the First Lady, Willow and Jaden Smith, and Selena Gomez and Justin Bieber, I've met a lot of A-list Hollywood celebrities and public figures like Olympic gold-medalist gymnasts Laurie Hernandez and Simone Biles, rapper Lil Yachty, actors Chloë Grace Moretz and Josie Totah, and many more. I never would have met any of these people if it weren't for the fame I gained from *Jessie*.

♥

One group of fans who have been extremely supportive of me are Black girls from all around the world.

First, there are not many parts for African American characters on TV. There are more now than there used to be, but so many roles are not open to Black and brown people. That makes those of us who have acting jobs super visible.

Even when African American girls get roles on TV and in movies, many of them have very light skin or are biracial. Very few are brown-skinned like I am, so a lot of brown girls, in particular, are big fans of mine.

It took me a while to understand that the same way I admire Raven-Symoné, some kids now looked up to me. It had never occurred to me that young girls would admire me like that.

Lots of kids say to me, "I really look up to you as a positive Black girl" or "I wanna be an actress like you when I'm older" or "You know how you did your fashion line? I wanna do that too." Parents of Black kids tell my mom, "You're doing a good job, Mom! Keep up the good work!" or "Your daughter's an inspiration."

It has been really cool to have young Black girls admire me, or try to wear the same hairstyles or dress the same as me. I'm excited to be a role model for them. I don't pretend to be someone else—I'm the best version of myself that I can be.

♥

Being famous has its good and bad sides.

On the good side, sometimes you get free clothes and makeup and other random stuff, and you get to do cool things.

But when you are in the public eye, you are basically giving your life away. Not always in a bad way, but your life isn't your own. You can't do the fun, cool stuff that you used to do with your friends, or at your school, or just walking down the street.

Having so many eyes on you can feel like a lot of pressure. You want to make sure you're doing everything right so other girls have someone to look up to. I would never want to do something that would make their parents say, "Oh, I don't want my kid watching her on TV or following her on social media." So I try to be myself, do what is right, and hang out with people who are genuine and have my best interests at heart.

A bad thing about being famous is that gossip bloggers are watching you 24/7, expecting you to slip up at some point so they can write the very first post about your mistake or share that Instagram video that gets them a kazillion likes but makes you look bad or ruins your career. Some are just waiting for that moment so they can write: "Your career is over." "We told you she wasn't perfect!"

Okay, yeah, a few child stars have gone wild or slipped up. But not everyone does. Plus, we are our own people. It's hard for the public to understand what it's like because they know us as our characters—they don't know us personally. Just like it's hard for some fans to see me as Skai rather than as my character Zuri. Not all kids who grow up in the public eye go wild, but we do make mistakes. They are probably similar to the mistakes you have made or will make. It just looks worse because we're celebrities. It makes us feel like we have to be perfect all the time. It gets a bit tiresome, and it's a lot of pressure.

I've seen kids have millions of followers, then do something stupid on social media, and seconds later their career is over, dead, and no one gives a darn about them at all.

So even though I did those stupid Vines, I learned so much from that experience. Sometimes it's still embarrassing. I'm like, "Dang, why did I have to do that?" But I was only twelve. A part of me doesn't regret it at all. If I didn't do it, I wouldn't have learned from it.

Even when you're minding your own business, crazy stuff can happen when you're in the public eye. Once, my hairstylist took an innocent picture of me sitting patiently with my legs crossed and my hands on my lap while I was waiting to be interviewed on *Good Day New York*. It was like six a.m. in New York, which means it was three a.m. in LA, so I had just been sitting there kind of nodding off when she took it. I ended up tweeting out the picture, and the next thing I knew, people retweeted it. Not only that, it became a meme! I guess the way I was sitting and the look I had on my face reminded them of someone being prim and proper. It started to symbolize how you look when you're being petty. Here are some of the funniest retweets:

"Him: I'm going out. Her: I know, that's why I got dressed."

"So you can tweet but you can't reply to my messages????"

"When you're cheating on a test and the teacher is walking around the room."

After people started retweeting it, I saw it on 3.14, my favorite meme account. I was like, "Oh my gosh, now I know it's really a meme if 3.14 reposted it!"

Since it was just funny, I encouraged people to make more memes. Then Shine On Media interviewed me about it and asked who I'd want to be in a meme with. I said Beyoncé, of course. Because, hello—Beyoncé! The next thing I knew, someone had created one with Kobe Bryant and Beyoncé: "When dad says no but mom says yes." It was so funny!

That said, it's really important to protect your reputation. Because whether you are famous or not, if you do things that give you a bad reputation, no one is going to take you seriously. The first thing they're going to do is type your name in a search engine, and the only thing that will come up will be silliness. In Hollywood, they won't want to work with you.

GROWING PAINS

When *Jessie* came to an end, we didn't know what, if anything, would happen next. We were hoping there would be a spin-off show. Disney is always looking for new shows, but we weren't certain they would continue the story line for our characters. Our fingers were crossed because we thought it would be fun to work together again. But then Disney asked Cameron to audition for another show on Disney XD, which is more geared toward boys. Hmm . . . that seemed weird. I guess it's not going to happen. That's life in Hollywood!

So I started going on auditions for other shows that weren't associated with Disney.

"Is your show over?" the casting director would ask.

"I don't know," I'd answer. "I haven't heard anything."

They knew that Disney had first say on my schedule, and if production started again, I would be unavailable until our next break. It could mess up their film.

As it turned out, Disney was planning a spin-off show called *Bunk'd.*

The whole premise of the story was that we would go to Camp Kikiwaka, in Maine, where our parents had met and fallen in love when they were teenagers. Our story lines would move away from all the glitz and glam, money and penthouses, nannies and butlers, to focus on a kids' summer camp experience. The *Bunk'd* set would have cabins and a lot of grass, just like at a summer camp. Our nanny, Debby Ryan, who by then was twenty-two; Kevin Chamberlin, who had played Bertram the butler; and the other grown-ups on *Jessie* weren't going to be in *Bunk'd*. It would be just us kids. All the kids but Cameron, that is. We were excited to get *Bunk'd,* but really bummed to lose Cameron. They wrote Cameron out of the script by saying that Luke stayed home.

Fortunately, one of the good things about summer camp is that there are lots of fresh faces and new friendships to make. During our first season, we added to our cast. There was Nathan Arenas, who played Jorge; Nina Lu, who played Tiffany; Kevin Quinn, who played Xander and became Emma's love interest; and Miranda May, who played Lou, the quirky, goofy camp counselor.

Because we'd had some time off, filming *Bunk'd* made acting so much fun again. My favorite episode centered around the character Tiffany. She wouldn't watch TV, fool around online, play with the other

kids—any of that stuff. At the camp, we were frenemies. In the episode, we introduced her to candy for the first time. Once she ate it, she was on a sugar high and acted like she was super hyper. It was the funniest episode we have ever filmed.

So the first season came and went; we had a good time and loved working with each other. We had the same characters for our second season as well, but by the end of season two, they wanted to revamp our show. The last episode was this cliff-hanger where the entire camp, the cabins, everything, burned down. Was it closing forever, or would we come back? It was so much of a nail-biter that *we* didn't even know.

Usually at the end of a season, you go on like a three- or four-month break. But then three months passed, then four months, then five months, six months, seven months . . . no answers. We were like, what the heck is going on? So just to be safe, we started going on auditions.

"Is your show over?"

"I don't know."

"Sorry!"

Dang!

Then Disney said they were going to revamp *Bunk'd*, but they didn't want to have any of the new kids on the show. That was disappointing—I loved those kids! But that's how it goes. The show was like real camp—not everyone comes back every year.

We got new faces, including Will Buie Jr., who played Finn, a kid from the country who was cousins with Lou, another country kid who was a counselor; and Raphael Alejandro, who played Matteo, an uptight kid who couldn't touch dirt. And then we had Mallory James Mahoney, who was Destiny, the princessy pageant girl who thought camp was disgusting until she learned to embrace it.

But season three got complicated. Remember my idol, Raven-Symoné? Well, Disney decided to pick up her spin-off show, which would be called *Raven's Home*. And she wanted to work on the same stage where she filmed *That's So Raven*—Stage 3/8, which was the biggest and best stage on the lot. We had to move to Stage 4. We also shared the same control room, and with those complications, things became a lot more challenging, and we had less time to shoot. Eventually, we worked out a plan where we filmed Monday and Tuesday instead of Thursday and Friday. There was so much going on, but we found a way to accommodate both shows.

Plus, after so many years of constant styling, my hair was getting damaged! So I decided to wear braided extensions in a box braid style.

When I showed up for the season with the extensions in, the producer and executive producer thought my hair looked great, but they said it made me look older. They wanted them to come out when we started filming. My mom told them that I wanted to keep them. Then, at the mixer before we started filming, a Disney executive loved them, thought the braids made me look younger, and said I should keep them. The producers said they would compromise. I could keep them in for three episodes, and then they would have to come out.

On top of that, the season three story lines were heavy. To explain our smaller campsite, they spun the plot as the owner running off with the insurance money. The season revolved around us convincing our parents to buy Camp Kikiwaka so they could rebuild the camp. Truth be told, I thought the story lines were still really funny. But some of the kids had never been on a TV show before, and they had to memorize a lot of lines. I felt so bad for them. I could relate to how they were feeling.

By then, I had played the same character, Zuri, for seven years. Though I loved her, I felt like I was outgrowing the role, and our schedules were a little tiring.

The entire last week of *Bunk'd* was my hardest acting experience by far. They wanted the final episode with the original cast to be the most unexpected. They had us in a hot-air balloon, but I got sick and couldn't keep up.

I was in so much pain, I could barely talk. At first, they told me I had strep throat, but then I got body aches. My back was hurting so bad, I can't even describe the pain. It felt like someone was cutting the bones out of my back. Then my fever went up to 104 and I was shaking and throwing up. I couldn't stand for five minutes, and I couldn't sleep. I would just cry. I spent a lot of time in my dressing room. But I kept working through it as much as I could.

Complicating things, Disney had worked it out for me to be able to shoot a pilot while I was also working on this episode, so I was doing acting double duty and I didn't want to delay either project. After we were done filming, I had to record voice-overs of my lines because I was so sick that I sounded like a raspy man.

Though a part of me felt sad that my time on the show was done and the original cast was all leaving, another part was excited to take on new challenges and opportunities.

By the time the third season of *Bunk'd* was over, I had really grown up and was ready to move on.

NO BULL-Y

If there's one thing you probably know about me by now, it's that I stand up to bullies. On the internet, I have become known for the "classy clapback," but I wasn't always like this. I've been bullied throughout my life.

Long before people knew my name, I got teased and bullied as a child. It happened many times in school, starting when I was seven years old. Back then, I would get bullied just for being short. I've always been the shortest person in my class, even going back to kindergarten. Some of the kids would be like, "You're so short," "You're a little mushroom," or "We could just step on you."

It made me feel insecure and would get me down. When I'd come home from school, I would tell my mom. One thing that's great about my mom, she's encouraged me to talk to her about anything.

My mom explained that some of the girls were probably jealous of me because I was famous. And even though I am short, lots of people are short. There's nothing wrong with that.

"If you wanna speak up for yourself, you can," she would tell me.

"Okay, I will," I told her. My mom has always taught me to stand up for myself. Even today, when we're walking down the street in New York and someone comes up to me and is too pushy, she knows what to say.

"And I'm not about violence or anything, but if someone hits you first, you can hit them back," she told me.

Fortunately, nobody did.

Sometimes all the teasing would make me cry. But when I cried, that would just make kids tease me more.

"You have a big nose."

"You're not cute."

I hated telling my mom negative news every day, but I knew that school shouldn't be like that.

"Skai, why is it every time I come pick you up, you always have a sob story?" she asked me. "What about the good stuff that's happening in school?"

I did have good experiences there, so I tried to focus on them. For one, there was my friend Layonie. She was really nice and always hung out with me. We would talk on the phone after school. Layonie was kind of like my backbone. But sometimes kids would tease her too.

As if the teasing wasn't enough, too many kids had been assigned to my classroom, so I was constantly turning around and getting distracted. It was also hard to focus on my schoolwork when I was getting bullied. On top of that, sometimes my friends at school would get cliquey. One week I would be hanging out with them, then the next some of the kids would isolate me and push me out or talk bad about me for no reason at all. When I became an anti-bullying activist, I learned that could be a part of bullying too.

"I really don't wanna go to this school anymore," I told my mom.

Then one day I came home with a scratch on my chest.

"How did you get that, Skai?" my mom asked me.

"Somebody pushed me at the water fountain and she scratched my neck," I said. It hadn't really hurt, but I still felt kind of scared.

That was it. My mom went to talk to my teacher about what was going on. The teacher understood but said she couldn't do anything about it. Right after that, I got the job working on *Jessie*.

BATTLING THE TROLLS

The next time I got bullied was when I started using social media.

After *Jessie* came out and I got my first Twitter account, it didn't take long before people started to say mean things to me.

"Don't you have a daycare to be at?"

"Why do you dress like that? It's hideous."

"You are so ugly!"

And some were way worse.

I was really surprised and hurt. *Whoa, what's going on?! Why are people I don't even know saying these things to me? What did I ever do?*

After I made my Instagram account, I would receive horrible comments on my photos.

"Hate your skinny body."

"You have Benjamin Button disease."

"I hope you die." I didn't think the death threats had substance, but even so, they were incredibly hurtful.

Plus, people would say very inappropriate things that I didn't understand.

I felt out of place, abused, ashamed, and exposed. Who were these faceless people? Being only nine years old and knowing that my mom had taught me to stand up for myself, I would reply back to them.

"You don't know what you're talking about," I'd reply. "Get off my Instagram." I would go off on them!

At first, responding to them felt good. I felt like I could control what was being said about me and repair it somehow by fighting the trolls. But after a while it started to feel overwhelming. I wasn't equipped emotionally to deal with it. My Disney advisers told me to stay away from the trolls. "If you give them energy, you're only feeding their power," they'd say.

I felt bad about myself constantly. I would stare in the mirror and wonder if I really was ugly. I would pick myself apart and wish that I looked like somebody else. I felt like it would never end.

My mom taught me that I should love the way God made me and that I don't have to respond to everyone that hurts me. But I was just a kid. It took me a while to understand that not everyone's opinion matters. The trolls didn't know me. They didn't have the courage to say things to my face.

BEING TRUE TO ME

The one thing bullying has taught me is to be comfortable with my true self.

First, I've had to be honest with myself about my height. I hated being short for the longest time. I didn't like being teased. It's a pain in the butt when my clothes have to be altered because I'm so small. I also look young, so it's like . . . UGH! It's especially hard during this time in my life when I want to look more mature. But then I see taller girls who wish they were smaller and skinny girls who wish they were curvier. So it seems like people always want what they don't have. It's taken me a while, but now I like my height.

Then there's my looks. There have been points in my life when I've felt like I'm ugly, even though at times people would tell me, "You're so pretty." Some days I think, "I wish I looked like her" or "My nose is too big and I need to wear makeup to cover it." There are times when I've wished I had this or that hair or skin color or body part.

Even when I haven't felt like I'm ugly, a lot of internet trolls thought

I was. They cyberbully me about my every feature and flaw, which can make me feel insecure. There are times when I go through that every day, and honestly, it is really hard.

I also know teenagers go through phases where they don't always feel great about themselves, and they don't love their looks. Plus, working in an industry that is so focused on appearances makes it more difficult—especially when beauty standards don't include brown-skinned girls. Maybe this should count as a type of bullying too.

Even when people think I'm pretty, at moments I wonder why they do. What's so special about me that fans want to look like me, yet when I look at myself I'm not satisfied? I realize that I'm in denial about my looks.

There are also those who think that I have this perfect life and who wish they could be me. People think that because I'm on television, I don't have the same insecurities as any sixteen-year-old girl. But I do. And when people bully me about them, it hurts. This industry tends to make you mature a lot faster than other kids do. So I am growing and learning how to be comfortable with myself. And I will get there when I get there. There's no rush.

I've spent a lot of time discussing these issues with my mom. She always reminds me to love how God made me. She also helps me understand that I'm only sixteen. My body's still developing, and my face is still developing. I am developing inside too, becoming a whole person. How I look now is not how I'm going to look in a year, five years, or ten years. And no matter how things turn out, I need to learn to love myself.

My mom has also helped me understand that lots of people are insecure, and everyone goes through difficult things in their lives. You never know what other people could be going through that may cause them to be mean or a bully.

These days I'm focusing on surrounding myself with high-quality people. I've changed some of my friends and have gained confidence from spending time with people who encourage me. I'm starting to feel like, finally, I've reached the point where I really don't care what anyone says about me. I know who I am, my mom knows who I am, my friends know who I am, my family knows who I am, and I've learned to let the negativity go over my head. That said, there are some days when I feel down, when I'm not happy with myself, and people just need to understand that. And sometimes negative comments do get to me. But it's important to remember that there are people who are going to support what I'm doing no matter what, and I have diehard fans, which I'm so thankful for.

FINDING MY VOICE ONLINE

As I've gotten older, I've started to find my voice. I've even become kind of well-known for taking on some bullies online. One of the most notable is the pop star Azealia Banks. Even back when I was ten years old, I would listen to her songs "1991" and "The Big Beat" all the time. Her beats are really good, and I connected with her just as a Black girl.

When I was fourteen, she came after Zayn Malik, who was previously

I'M LIVING FOR MYSELF.
I DON'T REALLY CARE ABOUT
WHAT ANYONE HAS TO SAY
NEGATIVELY TOWARD ME.

Skai Jackson ✋ ✔

@skaijackson

Azealia Banks needs to simmer down a little 👀 😂

6:49 PM - 10 May 2016

↩ 🔁 17,199 ♥ 31,964

in the group One Direction. I don't know Zayn personally and I don't know his exact race—I just know that we're both people of color. She attacked him with all sorts of racial slurs. I can't even repeat them, that's how bad they were.

So I took it upon myself to tweet, "Azealia Banks needs to simmer down a little." I didn't think it was that bad. I didn't even @ her to get her attention.

"I just tweeted at Azealia Banks." I told my mom I'd seen her go off on the internet before. It's like once she starts, there's no stopping her.

"What did you do?" my mom asked, then looked at my tweet.

"Oh my gosh, Skai, she responded. . . ."

Of course, it was foul. Azealia said that I have no boobs and no butt and I need to grow some hips. But I was only fourteen—I wasn't supposed to have big boobs and a big butt.

"Don't say anything," my mom told me.

"No, I'm gonna say something," I said.

"Skai, please . . ."

"No, really, I am."

Apparently, my mom forgot that she was the person who taught me to stand up for myself.

Then I started typing my response: "When a no hip having 14 year old has more class than you. Worry about your career. Get one ✌ "

Of course, Azealia didn't know when to stop. She tweeted, "LOL, says the Disney Channel Reject. . . . You know they don't like girls your color. Enjoy it while it lasts." And then, "lol ur mom's been pimping you out to disney since you were a lil girl. lets see what you end up like at 21. bye!"

She really should have stopped when she still had some dignity. And since the things she said about my mom were extremely uncalled-for, I thought, "Nope, I am coming back at you!"

I typed: "and I'm sure my mom did a wayyy better job then yours did! You give black women a bad name. I'll be praying for you." And then, "I had a career before Disney and I'm sure I will after! And I know I won't

turn out like you bitter and miserable! Fix ur life."

Then I got off my phone. The long list of people Azealia had a Twitter war with had grown longer: Nicki Minaj, Cardi B, me. I didn't want to give Azealia Banks any more of my time and attention. Plus, I thought her tweets were going to get really, really bad. And I worried that the feud would reflect poorly on me.

But that's not what happened. It turns out she got all the negativity. I got a lot of positivity. People tweeted supportive things like:

"A 14-year-old girl stood up to a 24-year-old."

"Wow, she really put her in her place without seeming disrespectful."

All of a sudden, people from MTV, a number of magazines, and many blogs started calling my publicist: "We need to do an interview with her!"

I was like, "Oh my gosh, what is going on? What did I do?"

But once I saw the positive reactions coming from it, I was really proud that I got to use my voice.

Many organizations also started reaching out to see if I wanted to do anti-bullying advocacy. I thought, why not use this opportunity to make a change for good? So I really started to preach anti-bullying and use my voice for change.

In the meantime, Azealia got kicked off Twitter for saying racially offensive things. And now nobody says, "Oh, yeah, Azealia Banks, her song '1991' was so good." Instead, they say she's out of control. Which is sad because she's a very talented artist. If she just focuses on her music, maybe some positive things will come to her.

I actually feel bad for her. Why aren't her friends telling her to get off Twitter or delete her tweets? Who is helping her get a proper support system?

I wish her some good help and better friends.

FIVE STEPS
TO COMPOSING A
CLASSY CLAPBACK

- **TAKE TEN DEEP BREATHS.** Never tweet while you're angry; you'll probably regret it later.

- **GET SASSY.** Never use curse words, foul language, or racial slurs, or say anything about a person's appearance. Just work with being smart-mouthed.

- **STICK TO THE FACTS.** See if you can educate them a little bit.

- **LESS IS MORE.** As in fashion and daytime makeup, go light. Say what you have to say, make sure you've been clear, then keep it moving. You don't have to use all 280 characters.

- **GET GHOST.** Type your reply, then turn off your phone or close the app and don't open it for at least forty-five minutes.

SCHOOL DAZE

By now you may be wondering how, in the middle of all the modeling and acting, I've been able to go to school.

To go all the way back to the beginning, because I was working when I was little, I didn't go to preschool like most kids do. My mom taught me how to count and how to read and write. We were always reading Dr. Seuss books: *One Fish, Two Fish, Red Fish, Blue Fish* and *Green Eggs and Ham* and more. One of my favorites was the If You Give a Mouse a Cookie series—I loved those books! *Goodnight Moon* was another one.

Between go-sees, we used to hang out in the big Scholastic store in Manhattan. We would be there for hours reading and playing with educational toys, like a doll where you opened up the shirt and saw the word *shirt,* or the word *zipper* next to the zipper.

When it came time for me to go to kindergarten, my mom enrolled me in a Catholic school because she and her sister had both gone to Catholic school. She liked the education she got there and thought it would be a good place for me. I was so excited and couldn't wait to start.

I remember the night before my first day of school, my mom ironed my white shirt and hung it next to the uniform she'd bought me. The next morning, she styled my hair into two ponytails.

"I'm nervous," I told her as she combed and brushed my hair.

"You're going to have fun and make new friends," she said.

Then she helped me with my backpack, and we walked to school together.

When we reached the front door, my mom pulled out her cell phone. She wanted to take a video of me for her best friend.

"Hi, I'm here, ready to go!" I said.

Then my mom gave me a kiss and a hug and watched me go in!

♥

Now, when my mom had signed me up for Catholic school, she'd told them that I was an actress.

"Oh, we don't tolerate that here, so don't even think you're gonna sign her up for this school," the woman in the front office told my mom when she mentioned that she might need to take me out of school to work or attend go-sees.

Wow, my mom thought, but she enrolled me anyway. When I would get work, she would make an excuse. One time my mom said I was sick. Another time she told me she would pick me up half an hour early.

"Do you have a note?" the woman at the front desk asked her.

"I'm her mom. I just need to pick her up early," my mom said.

"But do you have a note? You need a note."

My mom knew I couldn't stay in that school, so the next year she transferred me to P.S. 106. In New York, *P.S.* doesn't mean *postscript* like what you put at the end of a letter—*P.S.* stands for *public school.* There are so many schools in New York City that most of them have a number instead of a name. I went to Public School 106 . . . get it?

P.S. 106 was located in a section of New York City called the Bronx. Our neighborhood, Parkchester, had a Macy's, a Burger King, and a movie theater where we would go see five-dollar matinees. But P.S. 106 was a complete change from Catholic school. For one, the staff at P.S. 106

didn't give my mom a hard time when I had to be absent. I was the only person in the school in the business, and they were excited about my career. As long as I kept up with my classes, they supported me. But the classes were overcrowded, and a lot of them were held in trailers. Then we moved to Harlem, where I went to P.S. 36. The teachers and staff there were excited for me too. Occasionally a little too excited— that's where the Band-Aid incident in the assembly took place, and some of the girls started bullying me.

GOING TO SCHOOL, HOLLYWOOD-STYLE

Once we moved to LA, I went to school but not the regular way. I know, I know, when you think about actors and entertainers who are still just kids, you may imagine that we don't have to go to school or deal with homework. Sorry to disappoint you, but we do have to go to school on top of all our work. There are laws that protect child actors. One of those laws says that kids have to go to school for no less than three hours each day. Whenever I was on set and we were not filming or rehearsing, the other kids and I would drop our stuff in our dressing room, then go straight upstairs and go to school. On Monday through Wednesday, we'd usually get to work at eight a.m. for school. We'd do classwork for at least an hour, then head to the set when it was our call time. By law, we couldn't start work before nine a.m., and we couldn't work past nine at night. When we weren't filming, we would go to school.

Even though I did some of my schoolwork on set, I've gotten most of my education by being homeschooled. When you are homeschooled, you do all the work they would teach you in a normal school classroom at home by yourself, or your parent teaches you, or you do it online, or you hire a tutor. When you are working as a child actor, you can do some or all of those things, but you also have to do schoolwork on set. I'd do the rest when I got home and on weekends.

For fifth grade, I was enrolled in this school called Connections Academy. I did every subject online and only met my teacher in person one time, when I was tested at the end of the year. During the semester, I would talk to her over the phone, or email or live chat with everyone else in my grade. That ended up not being the best setup for me. I felt like I didn't have the one-on-one connection I needed with a teacher. So for sixth grade, I changed to a school called Opus Independent. It's located about thirty miles from my house and is mainly for kids who are working actors, although other kids go there too. I learn by reading books and listening to CDs on each subject. On top of that, I meet with my teacher once a week, either at my school for a couple of hours or somewhere else, like on the set. I've had Kate Thompson as my teacher

since I was in the seventh grade. She works with me and does binder checks to make sure I'm keeping up with my schoolwork.

When I was starring on *Jessie* and *Bunk'd,* we also had two teachers on the set, Cheryl Diamond and Jeri McBride. Their job was to help us through whatever curriculum we had. Ms. Cheryl would help me with math and science; Ms. Jeri was good at English and history. There were four kids on the show, and there were two classrooms. Two of us would be in one room and two in the other. Then

A SNEAKERHEAD ON THE RED CARPET

One thing I'm known for now is my style. But what I wear from day to day depends on if I'm going to a red carpet or just going about my everyday life.

My love of fashion started when I was three and my dad would take me to sneaker stores all the time. I'd always pick out boys' shoes, Nike Jordans. Don't ask me why.

Every time my dad would bring me back home, my mom would ask him, "Why are you always buying her boys' sneakers?"

"Those are what she picks out," he'd tell her.

"I want her to dress like a girl."

"I can't help it that she picks out boys' shoes."

My mom wasn't saying that there was anything wrong with boys'

styles. Back in the day, when she was growing up, my mom had a tomboy flair. She just wanted my dad to take me to a store where I could get girly sneakers or girly shoes, period. But I didn't want them.

"What a cute little boy," strangers on the street would tell my mom when they looked at me in my jeans and Jordans.

"I'm not a boy. I'm a girl."

When I turned seven, my grandmother bought me Jordans for my birthday. For Christmas, when people would ask what I wanted, I'd tell them Jordans. Even when I got older, when they'd ask about gifts for Christmas or my birthday, I'd say, "A new pair of sneakers or some money." Then I'd take my cash to buy some Jordans. I am one of the biggest sneakerheads ever.

I also like to wear boys' basketball shorts. They are so comfortable. And if you look in my closet, you'll see at least twenty kinds of hoodies. I get hoodies at concerts, people give me free hoodies, hoodies just come my way. I like to wear them 24/7, every single day.

"Can you put something else on other than a hoodie, boy basketball shorts, and Jordans, please?" my mom sometimes asks me.

"Okay," I'll say. Then I'll grab leggings, a hoodie, and fancy sneakers, of course. Or a graphic tee, shredded jeans, and sneakers.

I'M ONE OF THE BIGGEST

SNEAKERHEADS EVER.

I just don't care about my appearance, which is strange for someone who has been a child model, I admit. When you're famous, you're supposed to care how you look when you go out of the house. But I don't want to be bothered with having to wear nice clothes during the day. I'm a homebody, so I'm mostly inside anyway.

You might not recognize me if I'm not on the red carpet. You might walk right by me on the street. You will never see me wear heels on my days off. I'm not trying to put blisters on my feet or have corns on my toes just so I can wear some shoes. That's why I stick with sneakers and flats.

Unfortunately, in my closet I have three shelves full of heels—just heels. It kind of annoys me when I look at them because they should be full of sneakers.

FIVE SIGNS

THAT YOU ARE
A SNEAKERHEAD

I'd rather walk around wearing my sneakers than any designer shoe. But not everyone is cut out to be a sneakerhead. Here are some clues that you might be like me.

1. You are naturally drawn to sneakers instead of heels or flats or sandals.

2. You actually own a bunch of sneakers rather than just talking about owning them.

3. You know the names of all the different styles of Jordans, even back to the 1980s. You also know when the next Jordan style is coming out.

4. You've watched all the episodes of Complex's video series, *Sneaker Shopping*.

5. You have very rare sneakers, like the Eminem Jordans, which cost A LOT! This makes you an extreme sneakerhead, especially if they're the real deal—or you know that they exist!

♥

Now, on the red carpet, that's a whole different story. When you're on the red carpet, heels are nice. Heels make you feel special. And since I'm only five feet tall, they give me some height by making me five or six inches taller. But skip the stilettos. I prefer a thicker heel because they keep my feet from hurting quite as much.

One thing that helps when I'm wearing heels is the ballet lessons I've taken since I was a little girl. Ballet gives you strength in your core and helps you stand tall. It also makes you more graceful. People often

tell me that I have great posture and that I move fluidly. My ballet training is such a part of me that I don't even think about my posture until someone points it out.

So on the red carpet you may find me in the Giambattista Valli ruffled dress that I wore to the 2017 Red Carpet Fashion Awards. Or the black spaghetti-strap Red Valentino tulle ruffled dress and black Stella Luna ankle-strap sandals that I wore to the premiere of the movie *Christopher Robin*. Or the flower print Monique

Lhuillier dress I wore to the world premiere of *Ralph Breaks the Internet*. Or a canary-yellow Christian Dior sequined T-shirt dress and some black Aldo Lucia block heels with these amazing jewels on them that I sported to the Dior Addict Lacquer Plump launch party. You never know what you'll find me wearing!

When I'm going to an event, I let my stylist, Zadrian, know in advance. He sets the overall vision for my look, including my clothes, shoes, accessories, and hair and makeup. He also chooses the makeup artist and hairstylist and sends a breakdown of that vision to them. "Okay, this is the hair I envision for the look. I want the makeup soft. I want the eye dramatic."

Then he visits different showrooms to pull a bunch of outfits for me. Showrooms are places where designers put their clothes on display so buyers and stylists can see and buy them. Three or four days before the event, Zadrian will bring them to my house for a fitting. His assistant will come as well, and so will a seamstress. I'll try on the different clothes to see what looks I'm feeling or not feeling. Then I'll pick one outfit, and the seamstress will alter it to fit me.

Everyone shows up at my house on the day of the big event! Usually my hairstylist will come about three hours beforehand, depending on how difficult the style is going to be. I have a lot of hair and it's very thick, so it can take a while. Every now and then the style Zadrian envisioned doesn't work. When that happens, he'll have the hairstylist change it at the last minute. Everyone has to be very flexible. Then I'll get dressed and Zadrian will hand me my accessories, my purse, my jacket, or whatever else I'm going to wear. And out the door I go!

Red Carpet
ESSENTIALS

You never know what's going to happen when you're on the red carpet, so I always carry three things:

- **A LITTLE CLUTCH** to carry my phone and whatever I'm wearing on my lips.

- **POWDER** if I'm going to be on camera. Sometimes my skin can be oily, and that's how I manage it.

- **MY PHONE CHARGER.** I never know how long the event might be when my mom drops me off, and I need to be able to contact her.

SKAI STYLE

My love of fashion began when I was three, and I started to draw and design when I was four. I love to draw, though I don't do it enough. I started by creating my own dresses for Barbie. Ribbons, bows, all sorts of fabrics—nothing was safe from my fashionista eye.

After I moved to LA, one of my goals was to design my own clothes and sell them in stores so I could express my creativity and see other kids wear them. Then I got the opportunity to create my own clothing line. A company called Nowadays that was partnering with Macy's asked if I wanted to create a line with them for the holidays called Nowadays Skai. "Yes, I definitely want to do it!"

I had two meetings with them in New York. They showed me rough drafts of some of the ideas and options: pants, shirts, jackets, tights.

"Okay, this is what we're thinking about so far," they told me. They would suggest the style, fabric, and print. "Just give us your input," they said. Then I had the option of replacing the fabric with one I would want, or switching to different pattern options.

"Yes, I like this," I said about some of the items. "No, I don't think we should do that—too many sequins and sparkles," I would say as I channeled my inner tomboy. Or "I like the style, but I think instead of this color, we should do it this way." I wanted the clothing line to represent me as much as possible, though girls younger than me would be buying the clothes.

"Okay, we don't have to do it that way." The designers at Nowadays were really collaborative.

By the time we were done, there were more than twenty items of clothing, including shirts, sweaters, dresses, skirts, and jackets. All of my items were really playful, and girls could have fun wearing them. There were a lot of cool fabrics and patterns and textures. You could dress them up or down. They came in sets, but you could also mix and match, which is something I love to do. I was really happy with the final product!

There was a cute little silver-gray crop top with sequins on it and a shimmery, high-waisted full skirt that could go with it. I had skinny jeans that laced up like sneakers at the bottom and a black-and-white-striped top with cool stars on the back near the shoulders. That paired with a silver

bomber jacket with black stars on the front and contrasting black and white stripes at the neck and waist like a varsity jacket. One of my favorite items was this big, thick, velvety purple fur waist-length coat. It was so cute; you could dress it up and wear it out or put it over jeans and wear it anywhere.

Nowadays flew me to New York to attend Fashion Week and do a photo shoot wearing the line. That was surreal! *Teen Vogue* documented my experience by sending two people to take pictures and video of me at every show I attended. I had been warned that Fashion Week would be stressful, but I found it quite fun. That year I was wearing my own clothes, but I learned that designers lend celebrities clothes to wear when they go to their show.

I remember the day in October when the line launched. My mom and I went to the Beverly Center mall in Beverly Hills. In my imagination, I saw myself walking into Macy's and seeing a big poster of me wearing my styles. Well, that's not exactly how it went. Actually, it was kind of funny. We had to ask someone who worked there where the Nowadays Collection was. They were like, "Oh, I don't know," so we had to ask someone else. We went to the right department and you could see a poster of my face and my styles displayed together. They had all the jackets, tops, pants—everything from my collection.

"Wow, I really can't believe I accomplished something that I always dreamed of!"

We had gone during a school day, so it wasn't crowded. But a couple of women recognized me. "Wow, congratulations, that's very cool!"

Some of my items sold out, even online. They had to keep restocking.

My friends were really proud of me. "Now we can go to Macy's and get your clothes," they said. And since the clothes were also for kids a few years younger than me, their younger siblings wore them too, so that was really fun.

One of the best parts was when people would tag me on social media so I could see them wearing my clothes. Or when I would go to meet-and-greets, they would wear my stuff. That was really cool. I definitely would like to do that again! It would be great to have my own fashion line one day.

I went to New York Fashion Week again in the fall of 2018. Since my stylist has good connections with the brands, every show I went to would lend me clothes. They suggested four outfits, then I could choose. I went to three shows: Anna Sui, Escada, and Telfar, and I interviewed models and celebrities like Bella and Gigi Hadid on the red carpet for the Business of Fashion 500 Gala, which I also attended. My favorite outfit was an ivory suit with this amazing curvy black trim from Sara Battaglia. For fun, I wore my hair in a green curly bob.

Here's a funny thing about Fashion Week: the shows are very quick, not even ten minutes long. You sit down, the models walk the runway, and it's over. But I love going because of the creativity of the designs.

I REALLY CAN'T
BELIEVE I ACCOMPLISHED
SOMETHING THAT I ALWAYS
DREAMED OF!

The Perfect Outfit

I used to literally spend forty minutes just trying to pick out what I'm going to wear. But you can be very casual and plain and add good accessories to give you an edgy-chic look. Try starting with plain black pants, a black T-shirt, and a black jacket. Then add some accessories—interesting earrings, a great necklace, or a cool belt or purse—and decked-out shoes or dope sneakers. Aside from an amazing natural hairstyle, my top-three favorite accessories are:

- **EARRINGS.** I always have to put earrings on.

- **A BACKPACK OR A PURSE.** My favorite is my Louis Vuitton backpack or my little cute black backpack that I carry anywhere. I like backpacks more than purses because it's easier—you don't have to worry about setting it down, and it doesn't feel like someone can steal a backpack off of you.

- **A NECKLACE.** A necklace, earrings, and a cute bag really bring a look together. They're simple and classy, and you don't have to put too much thought into them.

PRO TIP: Go thrift shopping and buy something really cheap but interesting, then make it your own by cutting it up or adding patches to it. Suddenly you have the perfect casual, daytime look! You really don't have to put a lot of effort or money into your look.

THE THINGS I CAN'T CHANGE ARE THE REASONS YOU LOVE ME

As you already know, one of the most important elements of my style is my hair, which is usually twisted or twisted out. It's my signature style. I've become known for it, and I love it!

There was a short time when I didn't like my natural hair. For so long society and the industry only seemed to appreciate long, straight hair. And I have so many thick curls that it can be really hard to maintain. Just washing my hair, oiling it, and twisting it could take my mom three hours. I wanted to

get a chemical relaxer to make my hair straight. I thought that would make my life easier, and my hair would look like what society told me was beautiful. But when I used heat to straighten my hair, it completely damaged it and my mom said we were never doing that again.

For years, I have worked hard to get my hair healthy. When you model or are in the entertainment industry, people are always brushing, combing, and tugging on your hair. That isn't great even when they're not using product. When they are putting a lot of products in it, it can really ruin your hair, especially if the products have alcohol in them. If your hair is curly on top of that, forget it. By the time I was only five, my hair had already been damaged, even though my mom didn't allow stylists to use product. To try to fix the situation, she put a leave-in protein conditioner in my hair, but she accidentally left it in too long, and it made my hair fall out in the front. I had to wear thick headbands for a long time.

Most of my hair struggles came from working in a business where not enough people of different races are styling, and not enough people are educated about how to style and take care of Black hair, especially natural hair. It's really hard to have people who aren't Black setting the vision for how they want me to wear my hair. So often, Black actresses and models are expected to fit beauty images that aren't made for us. Some girls get pressured into wearing their hair relaxed, curly, and down. That's not who I am. It turned out that wasn't how my fans wanted to see me either. Me being curly and natural was best all around.

When you appear on a TV show, your hair gets styled and treated a lot, which can be really hard on anyone's hair—but is especially hard on natural hair like mine. It takes extra skill and care to keep my hair healthy. Plus, I really liked to try out different styles in my personal life but had to keep my hair consistent for my character's look.

So we came up with a great solution for everyone—a partial wig that would keep my character's hair looking consistent and great all the time without damaging my own hair. And when I was off set, I could experiment with new looks and express myself with my own style.

When I started the first season of *Bunk'd,* Disney hired my favorite hair stylist, Deborah Brown, who does an amazing job with natural hair. Ms. Deborah used to do the singer and actor Brandy's hair when she was on the show *Moesha.* She knew exactly what to do to restore and protect my hair without chemicals. She was also an excellent braider, and we tried a lot of fun new styles together.

My hair is very healthy now, and I'm not putting any heat or chemicals or anything on it to change it. On my off days, I usually wear it up in a bun so it's not in my face and I

don't have to deal with it. My hair is important to me, especially when it comes to different jobs and photo shoots. At this point I'm very strict about who I let style it.

A lot of Black girls are switching to natural hair. I love how so many of us are embracing what God gave us and taking pride in our natural curls, kinks, braids, and locs. Though we sometimes have to be patient during the growing-out stage to look the way we want, we like how we look and it shows. Black girls are wearing so many styles these days that a lot of people with straight hair wish they had curly or natural hair.

STYLIN' AND PROFILIN'

One thing I notice is that some girls seem to want to look like me. My fans go hard for me and love me—I am grateful for that. And if you want to say I'm pretty, thank you, that's nice, that's great. Especially because I struggle with insecurities and cyberbullies, it's nice to know that at least some people think I'm attractive.

But my mom always tells me it's more important to be beautiful inside. She has also taught me that it's essential to be kind as well as respectful. She taught me to say "please" whenever I want something, and "thank you" any time somebody does anything for me. Being polite and easy to work with has created many opportunities for me. I try to do this even when I'm having a bad day. To me it's a way to show your inner beauty.

I don't think anyone should try to be exactly like me. It makes you seem like a follower, and you should be your own person. God made you unique. If you are how God made you, that allows you to do something different from everyone else.

I also think that you should look like yourself. People often ask me for beauty tips, and my main tip is to express the beauty of you. But if you want to talk about beauty and makeup, here's my advice.

TIP #1: Less is more—don't wear too much. A lot of girls put so much makeup on. You really don't have to do that. Let your inner beauty shine through.

TIP #2: It's important to drink tons of water. I have very dry skin, so it's really good for me. To tell the truth, I really don't like it. Even though it's supposed to taste like nothing, no matter what kind of water I drink, it has a nasty flavor to me. But I've noticed such a difference in my skin since I started drinking it. One time, I was sick in bed for like two weeks. The doctor told me to drink lots of water. I noticed that all my little blemishes and marks went away. Wow, water can do all that?!

TIP #3: Take care of your skin. Clean your skin every night to get the makeup, pollution, and pollen off of it. I also put aloe vera or something natural on it so that it's healthy and glows.

TIP #4: Eat your vegetables. Not everyone likes the way they taste. But stick with them and you'll get used to it. Veggies help you have amazing skin!

FIVE BEAUTY PRODUCTS
THAT I CAN'T LIVE WITHOUT

Lots of people think you have to spend a lot of money for makeup or wear name-brand stuff. You really don't. I wear a mixture. Half of my makeup is from the drugstore for under $20. Here are my fab five.

- **HIGHLIGHTER.** The ColourPop brand in any shade really stands out to me because they are affordable. You can get their makeup for $10 or less, and it's very good quality. I use it all the time. I also use Rihanna's Fenty Beauty Killawatt highlighter. It has always been my favorite.

- **FOUNDATION.** Since my skin is so dry, drugstore foundations don't work for me—they leave my skin looking a little blotchy. They used Fenty Beauty's foundation on me when I attended Fashion Week in 2018. It's so natural, lightweight, and not full coverage. It makes your skin look like skin but just a little more perfect. When I do a photo shoot or red-carpet event, I use a high-quality foundation called Nars Natural Radiant Longwear Foundation. If you're getting your picture taken, you need more makeup so the flash doesn't make you look ashy or ghosty.

- **MASCARA.** Too Faced mascara is the bomb! I have really long lashes even without mascara, but Too Faced mascara makes my lashes look even longer. I wear it every day.

- **LIP GLOSS.** I use any lip gloss, even if it's from the drugstore. Maybelline, Too Faced, Benefit—any of it. Also any lip gloss that gives me a pop of color. I sometimes wear lip gloss in a neutral color.

- **EYE SHADOW.** One of my favorites is a Kylie Jenner palette. I like it because it's so natural. There are a lot of brands that I think do too much with palettes—they have all these bright blues and yellows and pinks. But I prefer a natural eye. ColourPop also has really affordable palettes that you can get at the drugstore.

FINDING MY VOICE AND TAKING A STAND

If there's one good thing about being an actress and in the public eye, it's that I get to have a voice and advocate for change.

One of the compliments I get often—whether from parents or kids or the media—is that I have found my voice and am not afraid to stand up for myself. People seem to admire me for that. Learning how to do that publicly hasn't been easy. I had to step out of my comfort zone.

When I was fifteen, a promoter who requests famous people to do meet-and-greets with their fans invited me to Little Rock, Arkansas, to visit a high school and give a twenty-minute speech in front of hundreds of students for Martin Luther King Jr. Day.

Now, I'd already done meet-and-greets, and I'd spoken for a few minutes in front of fans or at events. But, oh my gosh, the thought of writing such a long speech that I would make in front of so many people made my knees knock and teeth chatter like I was watching a scary movie!

I told you before that I'm a very shy person. When I was younger, I was talkative, all over the place and energetic. As I get older and more mature, I am more quiet and chill. If you meet me for the first time or don't know me well, it may seem like I'm shy. But if you get to know me, you'll find out that I'm very chatty and fun. Also, as a public figure, I have to be careful of the people I surround myself with to make sure that they're genuine.

I also have this weird thing when I'm reading. I don't know what it is, but I can't follow a sentence. Even in a book, I lose track of where I am or skip a line by accident or certain words flip around. I don't know if it's a mental thing or an eye thing. But reading in public is not my strong point.

Anyhow, the man invited me to speak about bullying in front of a gym full of kids at the school. *I am not doing that,* I thought at first. But I realized that if I wanted to have adventures and new experiences, I had to be willing to do new things that are out of my comfort zone. So I decided to push myself.

I wrote my speech and practiced it. And even though I worried that I would lose track of where I was, or the words would flip, or I would mess up a line, I kept going.

On the day of the assembly, I felt a lot of pressure. Not just because so many kids were there, but also because the governor and all sorts of important people from Little Rock were watching me too. What if I messed up?

"I'm really, really nervous," I told the man who had hired me.

"You'll be fine," he told me. "You're gonna go out there and have fun."

"I'll try."

"Don't concentrate on the negative; just concentrate on the positive," he told me. "Everyone's gonna love to see you."

So they introduced me, and I walked out onstage. When the audience started clapping, I smiled and relaxed a bit. Even though they didn't know how nervous I was, I felt like they were cheering me on. That definitely made me feel a lot more comfortable. #MyFansMean EverythingToMe #SkaiFansForLife

Then I paused for a minute, took a deep breath, and gave my speech. Somehow everything worked out.

As terrified as I was when I started, it ended up being a really good experience. Now I'm not afraid to do any kind of speaking engagement. If I hadn't done this speech, I probably would have been afraid to do all the other speaking events I've done since then.

As you reach for the sky in your own life, practice getting comfortable being uncomfortable and see what good things result!

♥

The MLK Day speaking event wasn't the first time I'd spoken in front of people, though the rest of my presentations had been much shorter or in front of smaller audiences. You see, because I stood up to Azealia

AS YOU REACH FOR
THE SKY IN YOUR OWN LIFE,
PRACTICE GETTING COMFORTABLE
BEING UNCOMFORTABLE AND
SEE WHAT GOOD THINGS RESULT!

Banks in such a classy style, kids started to look up to me in a brand-new way. Organizations like DoSomething.org, WE.org, and the Committee for Children have invited me to support their anti-bullying work, to help other kids find their own voice and bring that kind of harassment to an end.

DoSomething.org is a global movement that is getting young people all around the US and the world involved in making the world a better place. From donating jeans to homeless teens, to sharing fun little thumb socks to remind our friends not to text and drive, to convincing Apple to create diverse emojis, DoSomething.org is on the case. They invited me to film a public-service announcement against bullying. I talked about how so many kids get bullied because of the things that make them different, but we should be celebrating those differences instead. So we did a Treat Yo Friends campaign. To get involved, go to DoSomething.org/friends.

The Committee for Children invited me to film a PSA as well for their new campaign, where they introduced the bullying-prevention superhero Captain Compassion to help you find the words to use with your "bystander power" to stop bullying. Go to CaptainCompassion.org for tips, tools, and videos to help create a world without bullying.

Of course, I'm not the only kid who's been bullied. According to StopBullying.gov, 30 percent of American students in sixth through twelfth grade have experienced bullying, and about 70 percent of us have witnessed someone being bullied. Fifteen percent of high school students report being bullied online, but 55 percent of LGBTQ students report cyberbullying. Yet only 20 to 30 percent of students let adults know when we get bullied. We really need to make a change. If you're a boy, you're more likely to be physically bullied. Verbal and emotional bullying is more common among girls. If you or someone you care about is being bullied, I'm sending you love because I know how hard it is. It may seem like you're not going to make it through, but know that you aren't alone.

Even though it can be difficult, it's important to speak up about what's happening to you. Tell a family member, teacher, mentor, or friend, or your minister, youth leader, soccer coach, or the bus driver who takes you to school, so they can help you get the support you need. Don't hide or think that if you tell on the bully, nothing will happen or the bullying will get worse. If you feel like you're going to harm yourself, tell someone you trust or ask a parent to get you some counseling. Surround yourself with good people who believe in you and will uplift your spirit.

♥

In addition to my anti-bullying activism, I'm involved with other campaigns.

I was invited to write a speech and deliver it at the Los Angeles March for Our Lives to end gun violence. That day, so many streets were blocked off. We had to take an Uber to the event and then walk through thousands of people to get to the stage. That part was stressful.

The speech wasn't, even though I got to talk in front of thousands of people. Thousands!

When I spoke, I didn't think about how many people in front of me—I just imagined that there were one hundred. Afterward I was like, "Oh my gosh, I can't believe I just did that!" I'm really proud of myself because if you'd have asked me a year earlier, I would have said, "No, I can't do that."

I never thought I'd be given an opportunity to talk about such an important issue. I feel inspired by and really look up to the students from Marjory Stoneman Douglas High School. I can only imagine what they've experienced. That was such a traumatic event. It breaks my heart that this kind of violence has continued.

When I met some of the survivors, I couldn't believe what they lived through. I told them how proud I was that, in spite of everything they experienced, they could still be strong and fight. Many people wouldn't have been able to come forward against gun violence like they have. So it's very inspiring for me to see them using their voice to change the world. They even made an inspirational song titled "Shine," and they've performed it all around the world. I hope a tragedy like this can help the world realize how precious life is.

In addition to supporting an important cause, I got to show people that there is another side to me. I also got to present alongside a lot of my peers. Celebrities like Willow and Jaden Smith, Ariana Grande, Justin Bieber, and Kim Kardashian were there. It was such an exciting moment.

My speech was about how gun violence is terrible and we have to take precautions that we never had to before. We all need to create change and come together to make a difference.

Do you know about Red Nose Day? It's a movement led by the charity Comic Relief, which uses comedy to help end child poverty here and around the world. The organization partners with groups like the Boys & Girls Clubs of America, Charity: Water, Children's Health Fund, Feeding America, and Save the Children. Who wouldn't want to be part of that? So on Red Nose Day, I got to go to an elementary school and tour it with kids. We also played games together. Before I got there, a lot of the kids had written riddles. I read them out loud, and then we all had to guess the answer. Then we got to create jokes and stories as a group. You can buy a red nose and wear it on Red Nose Day to help raise money and awareness for child poverty. You can also go to RedNoseDay.org and learn how to hold your own fund-raiser and get your friends and family involved in a life-changing cause.

I also volunteer with an

organization called No Kid Hungry. At first, when I would think about kids not having enough to eat, my mind would go to an image of a kid in another country. But then I learned that kids are hungry right here in the United States, and even in California, where I live.

One out of every six American kids struggles with hunger. That means that at some point during the year, the kids or their parents don't have enough safe and nutritious food. The No Kid Hungry movement includes teachers, chefs, community leaders, parents, lawmakers, and CEOs who all believe that no kid in America should go hungry. You can help me spread the word at NoKidHungry.org.

My work with No Kid Hungry involves going to schools and leading Q&As or handing out school lunches. Lots of times the facilitators will ask kids about their assumptions. "If a kid came to school hungry, how do you think that would impact their day?" And the kids might say, "Well, I get very groggy if I don't eat breakfast, so I would be hungry and it would be hard to learn." Exactly!

And once I thought about it, I realized that could have been me. Though my mom always figured out how to make ends meet, she really struggled when I was little. We got government assistance for a short time to get us through. And we didn't always live in the best neighborhoods, so we were around a lot of people who were working hard but having a challenging time. I can only imagine how difficult that would be, going to school on an empty stomach. When I work and don't get to eat during the day, I get so angry, I'm not in the mood to do anything, and I don't want to talk. It breaks my heart to know that many kids go through that every single day.

I also help support the Children's Hospital of Los Angeles. Every so often I go there and read stories to kids who are in the hospital. I go to a cute little room where the kids who are feeling well enough can come. I get to meet them, talk to them, and read to them. I am not a super over-the-top reader. But kids get bored easily and I'm an actor, so I try to use a bit of my craft when I read. If there's a bear in the story, I'll growl. If there's a lion, I'll roar. I try to be a little bit extra and energetic with them. When people ask me what charity they should donate to, I always say Children's Hospital.

I'm also involved with an organization called WE, which helps regular people do amazing things in different communities and countries to improve the lives of the people there, and in turn change the world.

WE students raise money for charity, collect food for food banks, and do all sorts of wonderful volunteer activities. The organization saw that I am an anti-bullying advocate, so they invited me to come speak to kids on WE Day, and they flew me to a couple of different states to talk at arenas of thousands of kids who are do-gooders in their community. Kids don't have to pay anything to get in; they just have to contribute something positive to their neighborhood. I spoke in Seattle, Chicago, and New York twice about how kids can overcome bullying. Each time I speak, all the love and cheering from the crowd really touches my heart. Lots of the kids have been bullied or have even bullied other people, so they can

relate to the conversation. You can learn more about WE Day at WE.org.

In 2018, I hosted WE Day UN, an event at the Barclays Center in Brooklyn, New York, in cooperation with the United Nations. Angie Martinez, Sofia Carson, and Jenna Ortega were my cohosts. My job was to introduce the performers and talk about the importance of using your voice to stand up against bullying. The event honored do-gooders from around the world. We rehearsed the night before, which was my first time in the Barclays Center, the arena where the Brooklyn Nets play basketball. It seats almost 20,000 people—it's huge! We worked on two stages: a big one where the entertainers—Nas, Darren Criss, Sofia Carson, and others—performed, and a smaller one with a runway that extended out into the audience. This is where I spent most of my time.

On the day of the event, I met up with my cohosts in the green room to review the revised script. Then we walked the red carpet (which was actually blue!) so photos and videos could be taken. Celebrities like Nas, Sarah Michelle Gellar, and Kareem Abdul-Jabbar and public figures like Martin Luther King Jr.'s son Martin Luther King III attended the event. Since it took place on a school day, the kids arrived really early. By the time we went onstage, they were very energetic. Between the love I got from the crowd and having great cohosts, any nerves that I had vanished. Most of the kids were Disney Channel fans, so they all knew me when my name was called. Their cheers almost sounded like a roar! It was a great experience and confirmed that even though I'm no longer on Disney, many young kids still look up to me.

Get Busy

It's easy to get involved in a charity organization and help make the world a better place.

You can do simple things like **DONATING A DOLLAR** or **VOLUNTEERING** in your community. You can go on their website or call and ask how you can get involved. You can attend a **CHARITY EVENT**. You can help spread the news on social media. You can help your friends **UNDERSTAND ISSUES** that need more awareness in order to **CREATE CHANGE**. It's easy to do, and even the littlest things can make a big difference.

I've learned that I'm not cut out for every charity event. Recently I did a celebrity softball game. I got to hang out with a lot of famous people, like Quincy Brown, Ashley Greene, and Jamie Foxx, which was great. We all got to wear custom-designed uniforms, and my sneakers were amazing! I've never gotten to wear cleats before.

But it wasn't that fun. I don't play any sports, and I didn't know how to play baseball at all. I was so bad that I didn't know that when you hit the ball, you're supposed to run. So I, of course, was tagged out. And when my team wasn't batting, they had me playing in the outfield.

I didn't even know where it was. *Can someone please tell me where to stand? How embarrassing!*

Plus, I have a fear of catching balls. When I was younger, I got hit in the nose with a basketball and my nose almost started bleeding. Ever since, I get scared when a ball is flying toward me. Good thing there were other people on my team. When I saw a ball coming my way, I just moved. It was too stressful. I started sweating.

Everyone was like, "Oh my gosh, you have such a good spirit about it." But on the inside I really couldn't wait for the game to be over. I was nervous the whole time.

I also participated in a First Tee golf event. They didn't tell me I'd

actually be trying to play indoor golf. I had heels on, and when I swung, I barely touched the ball. My ball went three feet, and other people's flew like sixty feet.

"Why don't you take off your heels?" they told me. So I took off my heels, but it didn't help.

I never want to play a game again where there's a ball and a bat or a ball and a stick or a ball and a racket—not even tennis, and I met Serena Williams at Arthur Ashe Kids' Day. At least I met J. R. Smith, a famous basketball player for the Cleveland Cavaliers. #GoCavs?

HONORING TWO CHAMPIONS

Speaking of Arthur Ashe Kids' Day, in 2018, I was invited to cohost this family festival that takes place right before the start of the US Open—one of the four most prestigious tennis tournaments in the world, which are called Grand Slams. Arthur Ashe was a famous tennis player and humanitarian who helped to integrate the sport. He was the first (and remains the only) African American male tennis player to be ranked number one in the world and the first African American man to win the men's singles championship at Wimbledon, the US Open, and the Australian Open—three of the four Grand Slams. Around fifty years ago, he started the National Junior Tennis and Learning Network (NJTL) to provide free or low-cost tennis to children who might not be able to afford to play. Today, NJTL serves 225,000 children each year, and Arthur Ashe Kids' Day (AAKD) helps to fund it.

I had two days of rehearsal before the event, when I got up at seven a.m. to get ready. On the first day I wore a Ralph Lauren pettiskirt and a polo shirt with my birth year on the back.

There were two different sets for the event. I was on the elevated stage, and my cohosts were on the tennis courts. My job was to introduce the performers and presenters, and then interview them afterward. *What does it feel like performing here? Is this your first time? When is your new music coming out?* That kind of thing.

Arthur Ashe Stadium holds 49,000 people, and it was completely full. The crowd was screaming and cheering, especially for Serena Williams. She and a number of other tennis superstars—Rafael Nadal, Novak Djokovic, Angelique Kerber, and Madison Keys—played exhibition matches for fun and had a skills competition.

I got to introduce Serena Williams and ask her several questions. I was excited to be in the company of this brave, powerful Black woman who is such a great role model for all of us. Serena is a trailblazer for Black women in tennis and gender equality in sports. I found being in her presence to be very empowering.

MEETING THE LION KING

After I'd participated in many speaking engagements for WE, they invited me to go to Kenya with them. Wow! I'm so grateful that they thought of me for such an incredible opportunity.

My trip to Kenya was with an arm of WE called Me to We and was my first time in Africa. Me to We helps people shift from "me" thinking to "we" thinking, whether shopping at the store and considering your environmental impact or making change around the world. About ten of us went: my mom and me; my good friend Jenna Ortega, who acted on Disney, and her mom; and several other child actors and their families. So first, let me say that Kenya is really, really far away. It's literally 9,600 miles and took like twenty hours to get there! It was the longest trip I'd ever taken in my life. My mom and I left out of Los Angeles. Our first flight was from LA to Istanbul, which is in Turkey. That flight took about thirteen hours. It was a red-eye, which means we left in the evening and flew overnight. A little bit after we took off, they served us dinner and dessert, then I went to sleep. I woke up at like seven in the morning, then they served us breakfast. We landed shortly after we finished eating breakfast, but it was dinnertime in Turkey. It was also totally the next day of the week. Time flies when you're on a long flight.

Next, we flew from Istanbul to Nairobi, the capital of Kenya. From Turkey to Kenya was only about six hours. That wasn't bad. I just watched a couple of movies and next thing I knew, we were there.

We stayed overnight at Hotel Hemingways, a luxurious hotel in Nairobi. Then the next day we flew on a little plane to the Maasai Mara,

an enormous national park that's world-famous for its lions, leopards, cheetahs, and huge migrations of zebras, gazelles, and other animals. The first thing I remember when we got off the plane was that it was extremely hot. It was a dry heat, kind of like California. You felt it as soon as you walked off the plane. But it was drier than California, and it wasn't as green. We weren't at a big airport like we were in Nairobi—the landing strip was dirt. A car was there waiting for us. When we started driving, we saw a lot of animals right away: monkeys, zebras (I hadn't seen a zebra that close before), pretty much anything you could think of. That was an eye-opening experience.

We all stayed at this place called Bogani Cottages. My mom and I stayed in a big cottage that looked a lot like a house. It had three bedrooms in it, and a loft upstairs. We had five beds. We were thinking, "Oh my gosh, if we had known, we could have brought other people and filled the space up!" The cottages were decorated with African fabric and accessories. But it was the opposite of our stay at Hotel Hemingways. There was no Wi-Fi. We had showers, but they had to boil the hot water for us in these big tin barrels. We could see fire beneath them, and then the water would flow to our room through pipes.

We had been invited on the trip to see WE's work there—to see how they've helped villages develop as far as building wells, schools, and hospitals.

One day during the trip, we went to several schools that WE helped build. We went to a school with younger kids, an all-girls high school, and a WE College for girls who want to go into the medical profession.

I got to visit classrooms and talk to the kids. One of the things I learned was that the schools they used to go to before WE got involved had been built out of mud. They didn't always have a roof. If it rained, their classrooms would kind of melt down to the ground. With WE's help,

they have been able to build classrooms with walls and a solid roof and windows so the students could get the best education possible.

At the high school, all the girls wore the same uniform and had the same short natural Caesar haircut. They looked very polished.

It was a boarding school, which means they moved away from their community, lived at the school, and only saw their family on breaks. Most of them don't live close enough to travel home on weekends. One girl hadn't seen her family in three months, but she knew they had sacrificed for her to get a great education. She missed them, but she loved school and realized how important it was. They were able talk to them on the phone if they had one. And every two to four months, they got to go home to see their parents. All in all, the girls seemed very happy.

If that was me, I'd be sad. But I think I'd also realize that my mom was doing it for an important reason, to give me a good education. I know that I would be okay if I could at least talk to my mom once in a while.

We also got to see the girls' daily routine. Their lives are really structured, and their days were planned out from morning until night. They wake up at four in the morning and arrive at school at 4:50. So early!

I am not a morning person, so I could never make that work. They walked us through the school and showed us their classrooms, their science experiments, these really interesting mini-robots they made out of Legos. I'd never seen something like that. And when they connected them to their laptops, the robots could move. It was so cool! Then they talked to us about the classes they take. They're basically the same classes we have in the United States, but they take a lot more of them.

During their typical day, the girls break for thirty minutes for lunch and thirty minutes for dinner. They also do activities during the day. For instance, they play volleyball and football—their football is our soccer—for ninety minutes every day. They were really good.

At eight p.m., they start doing their homework. Their school day doesn't end until ten p.m., then they start all over again in the morning. Imagine being up from four in the morning to ten at night. American kids go to school for seven hours each day, and we complain about it. These girls work ten times harder than we do. It was amazing to see.

Even though we live very different lives, the girls and I had a lot in common. They love music and listen to many of the same artists we do, like Nikki Minaj, Cardi B, Rihanna, Drake, and Remy Ma. I also got to listen to some of their music. A number of the dances were very similar, and they even knew some of our dance moves.

When it came to food, the girls kept asking me, "Oh, have you tried this?" And I would try it and like it. Several of the African flavors even tasted familiar.

While we were there, we also helped to build a medical center. Oh

my gosh, the work was so hard. First, we had to fetch our own water in barrels. There was a twine rope that held the barrel, and we put it over our head. The barrel would rest in the curve of our back. We filled them with up to fifty pounds of water, then carried the water for almost a mile. Let me just tell you: that was not fun. I had to hold my head a certain way so I wouldn't hurt myself. We met a woman who told us that when she was building her house, she sometimes had to take that trip thirty-six times a day, with fifty pounds of water on her back and a twenty-five-pound baby on her front. I was sooo tired after *one* time. I learned that women are trained to carry water when they are little girls. Their bodies adapt to it. The experience gave me a lot of appreciation for my own life.

When we got back to the medical center, we helped them build some walls. Well, we tried, that is. It was a lot harder than it looked. We had to mix the plaster a very specific way. Then we scooped it and flicked it against the wall with our wrists so it stuck. Then we smoothed it. Well, the guides, who were Kenyan, were doing it perfectly. When we tried to do it, we couldn't make it stick. It would just fall down.

After we were done for the day, we would go back to our hotel and have dinner. Every day we ate something different, and the food was amazing. At night, all the WE volunteers had time to talk. We would discuss our favorite part of the day and share our thoughts and experiences. Then they'd tell us what we were going to do the next day. My favorite activity was making beaded bracelets with the mothers—we called them Mamas—who WE works with. They pay the Mamas to make bracelets, which are sold to make money.

About four days into our trip, we got to go on safari. I was really excited to see animals! We rode around in a big bus-type thing with open windows but high sides. Before we took off, they warned us not to get out of the bus or to stick our hands or legs out of the window. Even though it doesn't happen very often, it's possible to upset an animal. They didn't want anyone getting attacked. That was a little scary!

We drove around for hours. They told us to be on the lookout for the big five: elephants, lions, leopards, buffalos, and rhinos. Those were the most dangerous and difficult animals to catch, back when people hunted on foot. We saw all of the big five except a rhino, which we didn't see until we visited an animal sanctuary later in the trip. My favorite part was when we saw a family of lions—a mother and a father and two babies. We got really, really close. That freaked my mom out!

Along the way we also saw giraffes, antelopes, zebras, cheetahs, hippos, baboons, and rheboks. Because I'm such a sneakerhead, I thought rheboks were just a shoe. Now I know where the name comes from! It was amazing to see animals I'd only ever seen in a zoo. All the animals seem much livelier in the wild. Like elephants—in the zoo, they just kind of stand there. When you see them in the wild, it's kind of shocking how much faster they move! We were also keeping our eyes open for the animals they call the ugly five: wildebeest, warthogs, vultures, marabou storks, and hyenas. We saw only one hyena, walking by itself. It was kind of scary-looking. Yeah, it was really ugly!

During our trip, we had two guides for all our activities. One of them, Easy, dressed like an American. Our other guide, Wilson, was a Maasai warrior. He wore traditional Maasai garb, which looked like thin

blankets draped over his shoulders. Instead of pants, he wore something that to us would look more like a skirt. He was also wearing these amazing beaded earrings that Maasai warriors wear.

If you don't know anything about the Maasai people, they are nomads who raise cows. They live mainly in Kenya and Tanzania. The first thing you notice about them is that they are very tall. Like really tall.

Maasai warriors were feared fighters. Wilson taught us some of the things they have to do, starting when they are little boys. One of the most important things they have to learn is how to deal with pain. A Maasai warrior can't show pain—ever. So the men do things like scrape boys with the thorns from acacia trees. When the boys are around eight years old, the men take out their two bottom front teeth without novocaine. Ouch!

Handling the pain is a sign of strength to them. I can't even manage a paper cut.

When they're a little older, the boys learn how to stalk and spear a lion by themselves. It shows that they're strong and that they can go up against a huge animal with barely any weapons. It's basically they die, or the lion dies. If the lion dies, they get to keep the lion's mane and put it in their house, and the other Maasai warriors get to keep the tail as a symbol of the victory. He's a true lion king.

I don't personally enjoy hunting animals. But I know in other cultures it's a way of life, either for food or a rite of passage. For the Maasai warriors to have the strength and courage to risk their lives—I really respect that. I mean, if it was me or the lion, I would have to try to kill the lion. But I definitely would not like to do it.

Another really interesting thing I learned is that the men don't know how old they are. They were born in small villages where they didn't use Western calendars. When Wilson asked his mother how old he was, she told him he was two hundred. Hmm . . . two hundred what? But he wasn't sure. He decided that New Year's Day would be his birthday, and he celebrates it every year.

Traveling to Kenya made me see my own life differently. Many of the people we met had just a few material things, but they all had such positive energy. It made me realize how many more clothes, gadgets, and electronics I own in comparison. I take a lot of my possessions for granted. But the people I met seem to be a lot happier with less. I'm learning the value of simplicity.

I had a great time in Kenya. If I get a chance to go again, I want to take some of my friends. I think everyone who has the opportunity should visit Africa. It was amazing being outside of California and learning about other people's lives.

TEAM BROWN SKIN

There's another topic I want to talk about, and I admit that it's kind of awkward.

No one wants to say out loud that they believe people of different races or backgrounds aren't beautiful. Nobody wants to make themselves look bad or seem racist or anything negative like that.

But the more I'm involved with acting, modeling, and entertainment, the more it seems like lots of people have trouble seeing that Black girls and women are as beautiful as white girls or girls of other backgrounds. And some people seem to have even more trouble seeing Black and brown girls' beauty when they have medium-brown skin, like I have, or dark-brown skin, like so many other girls do. I don't know why.

This preference for light skin is known as colorism, and I deal with it every day. Colorism involves discriminating against people who have darker skin colors, whether they are African American, Mexican American, Nigerian, South African, Pakistani, Brazilian, or another ethnicity.

Being involved in modeling and acting, you see a lot of casting calls where only white people are considered for certain jobs. So that means that actors of color get fewer opportunities, which means we end up competing against each other. When there are roles for Black characters, you often hear that they're looking for actresses with a biracial appearance. What they really mean is a very light skin color, more European features, and long curly or straight hair.

Now, there are many beautiful and talented girls with light-brown skin and long curly hair whose work I admire. But when there are so few girls with medium-brown or dark-brown skin getting roles, it's easy to wonder what's going on. Why are darker-skinned girls not good enough?

When I started out as a model, you didn't see a lot of African American girls doing magazine ads or acting on television or in movies at all. That's why Raven-Symoné was so important to me. I saw her doing something I wanted to do, and it's hard to be what you can't see. Seeing someone who looked like me with her own television show made me think I could be an actress. That's one reason why it's important for people of all backgrounds and skin colors to be given opportunities.

Today, because brown-skinned girls are not used to seeing a lot of models and actresses who look like them, I'm told all the time that I've become a role model for them. It's exciting to know that I inspire them. But there needs to be more roles for brown-skinned and dark-brown-skinned girls.

I don't even consider my skin dark. There are girls who are much

TO ALL MY
BROWN-SKINNED SISTERS
OUT THERE, KEEP CHASING
YOUR DREAMS AND KEEP
YOUR HEAD UP.

darker than me in the industry, and I can only imagine how terrible this must make them feel. There shouldn't be a #TeamLightSkinned or #TeamDarkSkinned. We need to make more roles available to everyone. Our industry needs to change. To all my brown-skinned sisters out there, keep chasing your dreams and keep your head up. Change is coming, and I see you.

To all of my fans of other races, please be good allies and friends so that everyone can have a fair chance.

Black Girls
ROCK!

Even though our contributions often get overlooked, brown-skinned girls and women are doing amazing things. Here are twenty-one Black women who inspire me.

CHLOE BAILEY

ANGELA BASSETT

GRACIE MARIE BRADLEY

NAOMI CAMPBELL

LAYLA CRAWFORD

VIOLA DAVIS

RYAN DESTINY

WHOOPI GOLDBERG

IMANI HAKIM

COCO JONES

LESLIE JONES

NATURI NAUGHTON

LUPITA NYONG'O

KEKE PALMER

RIHANNA

AMBER RILEY

ANIKA NONI ROSE

GABRIELLE UNION

QUVENZHANÉ WALLIS

And who can forget **MICHELLE OBAMA** and **OPRAH WINFREY**?

MY #RIDEORDIE AND MY PEEPS

In order to make it in this business, it's really important to have a great team.

One of my most important relationships is with my mom. She sacrificed so much for me, and without her, I wouldn't even be an actor, following my dreams. I also wouldn't be living in Los Angeles—I'd still be in New York, and you wouldn't know who I am.

My mom put her own dreams of being a dancer aside so that I could have a better life. She also put her chance to go to college on hold. For a while, she would leave me with a babysitter and take classes at night, not getting home until eleven. Sometimes I had to be on set at eight a.m. She had to get us both up, feed me, dress me, do my hair, and get me there on time. By then, I had become one of the most popular African American

child models, so I was working almost every day. Going to school while getting me to go-sees and auditions was just too much for her. So she had to make a choice, and she chose me. #RideOrDie

Sometimes I compare my life to my mom's when she was my age. Even though she had to move out on her own and grow up more quickly than most, if that didn't happen she wouldn't be who she is today. Life has taught her so much about how to hustle and struggle to get what you want, and she has taught that to me. Like I said before, sometimes you can even learn from the things that make you feel uncomfortable.

I also really appreciate my mom because she listened when I told her acting was a passion of mine. I was hungry for it and really wanted it—I was lucky that she allowed me to follow my dreams at a very young age. And even though it took six or seven years to make a name for myself, it all worked out in the end. If she wasn't willing to struggle and be such a go-getter for my dream, I wouldn't have had these amazing opportunities. I'm glad I've received my kind personality, can-do attitude, and strong work ethic from my mom.

As I meet more people and hear their stories, I realize I was very fortunate to have a mom (and manager) who is so accepting of what I want to do with my life. It's been me and my mom for sixteen years, and I wouldn't trade the memories we've made together for anything in the world. She's my best friend.

ONE OF MY MOST IMPORTANT RELATIONSHIPS IS WITH MY MOM. SHE SACRIFICED SO MUCH FOR ME, AND WITHOUT HER, I WOULDN'T EVEN BE AN ACTOR, FOLLOWING MY DREAMS.

HOW TO

CONVINCE YOUR PARENTS TO LET YOU PURSUE YOUR DREAM

STEP 1: Explain to your parents why this is something you really want to do.

STEP 2: Prove to them how dedicated you are by getting involved in activities that will help you practice your craft.

STEP 3: Even if they say no, keep chipping away at it on the side so you can get good at it over time. I have so many musician, rapper, and actor friends whose parents told them no, but now they see them successful and are like, "Oh, I made a mistake."

♥

And I don't want to take anything away from my dad. My dad was around sometimes, then for a while he wasn't in my life at all. When I was little, I remember he would pick me up on weekends and we would go out. He'd always take me to Toys "R" Us in Times Square—that was a really memorable place for me, with all its bright, flashing, colorful lights and billboards. He was a fun person, but my dad was stricter than my mom. And there were times when I would cry and want to go home because I was just used to my mom and didn't know my dad well. I was with her every day, so it was hard being with someone new. It took a long time for me to get comfortable around him and even call him Dad.

Then, two years before I moved to LA, my dad married my stepmom, Opal. She has always been so nice to me. I was excited to go to my dad's house to see them together. She is a teacher and would help me with my schoolwork.

"All right, let's get you prepared for third grade," she'd say.

I was thrilled when my dad got married and I also became a big sister. I was still living in New York when my

first little sister, Aurora, was born. But we moved to LA when she was only about eight months old, so I didn't really get to see her grow up. Three years later, I got another little sister, Nala. I try to visit them when I go back to New York. The sad thing is I'm rarely able to make the trip, so I've met my younger sister only two times. But she is such a sweet girl, and I FaceTime them all the time. I want to be in my sisters' lives and teach them things, but it's hard being so far away.

Even though my dad and I drifted apart for a while, we got a fresh start and he's in my life now. I talk to him every day, we call each other and text, and I see him whenever I have the opportunity. It's been really fun getting to know him again.

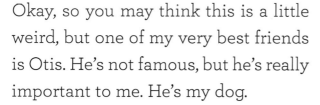

Okay, so you may think this is a little weird, but one of my very best friends is Otis. He's not famous, but he's really important to me. He's my dog.

I got Otis when I was filming *Jessie.* Back then, I was just getting over my heartbreak from having to give away my other dog, Chester, a little dark chocolate mutt who was only around ten pounds. We got Chester to keep us company when we moved to LA, but he was a rescue dog and had separation anxiety. Whenever we would leave our apartment, he would bark a lot, tear the windows up, and pee everywhere. Once, he peed on a bunch of our clothes. We had to give him to someone who had another dog so he wouldn't feel so lonely.

Then one day they spread the word at the studio that they were going to have a dog shelter visit the studio lot. All of these dogs arrived in RVs. I really, really wanted another dog. But my mom wasn't sold. "I don't know if we're gonna get a dog."

Until we saw Sammy.

One of the ladies who had organized everything told me, "We're gonna have this dog Sammy come, and he will be up for adoption." Sammy was a West Highland terrier, white and well groomed, like the dogs you see in commercials. As soon as I saw him, I wanted him. My mom loved him too. So did everyone else! They all wanted him.

"You can't have Sammy," the lady said.

"I don't understand what you're talking about," I told her.

"He stops when you're trying to walk him," she said.

"I don't care," I told her. "I just want him."

I think she just realized that everyone wanted him, so she decided she wanted to keep him.

"I'm gonna give him to my boss," she said. "Go look at the other dogs."

"But I want him," I said. I was just ten, and by now I was crying.

"Let's go look at the other dogs, Skai," my mom said.

That's when I saw Otis.

Otis looked like a mess when I first saw him. He was white and black and had really long hair. He had a cold, so he was sneezing and coughing all over.

"I do *not* want this dog," I told her.

At the time, I didn't think he was cute. Then again, who's cute when they are sniffling and have a cold? Plus, he hadn't been groomed, so his hair was matted and sticking out all over the place. On top of that, he was wearing a diaper. Seriously! A dog diaper. He needed it because he was being locked in cages all day and they didn't want him to have an accident.

"I don't want him," I told my mom. I couldn't see how this sneezing ungroomed dog could ever be as cute as Chester.

"We'll take him," my mom said. My mouth opened wide, but nothing came out.

"You can just do a little trial with him," the man from the dog-adoption agency said. "If you don't like him, you can always bring him back."

So we adopted him and were told his name was Oreo.

"What should we name him?" we wondered.

My mom's friend gave the suggestion of Otis. "That's a cute name!"

Now, I don't know what my mom saw in Otis. But she can tell when something has potential. She knew that if we took off that diaper, gave him a bath, took him to get a haircut, and gave him some love, he could be part of our family.

At first, Otis, who is a Chihuahua terrier mix, was traumatized. He

didn't eat, he didn't use the bathroom, and he still had his cold. Then the second day, the same thing. Okay, this is weird. What's going on? That's when I stopped thinking so much about Sammy and started thinking more about Otis. I felt sorry for him. After about a week, he started to get used to his new surroundings. That's when we took him to get groomed. He still had a cold, but he looked cute when he got a haircut. I learned that he was very shy. And he didn't bark or anything.

But the cold didn't go away for like a month. He would hack and cough so hard that it sounded really nasty, almost like he was choking. So we were like, "Okay, this can't just be a cold." We took him to the vet, and it turned out Otis had an infection and he could have died. We had to put pills in his food and try to talk him into eating them. Eventually he started taking them and got better.

As I got older and spent more time with Otis, I realized what a good dog he is. He's really smart. I've never seen a dog that smart. It's like he understands what I'm saying, and it's kind of eerie.

He's now seven years old, but he still acts like a puppy. I'm so glad we gave him a chance. He's an important part of the family and is always there to come home to and watch movies with me. He adds so much happiness to my life.

I THOUGHT I KNEW MYSELF. SOMEHOW YOU KNOW ME MORE.

My friends are a big part of my life. When I lived in New York, I used to spend time with my friend Layonie. But we fell out of touch when I moved to LA.

In LA, I used to have a lot of friends, but I felt like I had to cut some people out of my life. I don't have many friends right now, and that's my choice. The friends I have, most are regular kids, and I try to hang out with them as much as I can.

Mostly, we do regular teenage stuff. We go to The Grove, which is a mall, or Fairfax Avenue or Rodeo Drive in Beverly Hills, just to walk around and look in stores. We also like to go to the movies.

We often go to Melrose Trading Post, a market where vendors sell all kinds of things, including vintage clothes. Sometimes I'll get my clothes from there because they are fun and different from what you see at the mall. They reflect my sense of style. You probably know by now that I also love to go to sneaker stores. Or we'll hang out at my house, where we'll get in the pool or hot tub, and then just chill and watch movies.

One of the things I really like about my friends is that it never bothers them when people come up to me to take pictures when we're eating or at the mall. They never ask me why I have to take so many pictures. I'm lucky to have a squad that's so understanding and always has my back.

I'M LUCKY TO
HAVE A SQUAD THAT'S
SO UNDERSTANDING AND
ALWAYS HAS MY BACK.

One of my very best friends is Josie Totah, who used to guest star on *Jessie*—Josie played Stuart, a boy who had a crush on Zuri.

Recently, Josie came out publicly as transgender. But about a year before, she told me that she was on hormones. She felt like she was a girl on the inside, even though her outer shell was a boy. It was special to me that Josie trusted me enough to tell me that she was going to go through this transition. I'm really proud of Josie because at seventeen, she's inspiring transgender kids to embrace who they are.

When I expressed my support for Josie right away, I started getting

comments like "How do you say you believe in God?" on social media. Obviously, God made us all a certain way. When God made Josie, He knew who she was. He knew her path. I think God loves you no matter what. Plus, I feel like everyone should just stop with the hate. I'd rather a person be happy with themselves than be depressed because they can't be who they are inside.

BLUE SKIES AND BEING RECOGNIZED

etween graduating from my many years at Disney, growing to become a youth activist, and recently getting my driver's permit, the last couple of years have been amazing for me. It seems like all the hard work I've been doing to be a role model and use my voice to help others is getting noticed.

In 2016, I was nominated for an NAACP Image Award for Outstanding Performance by a Youth. I didn't win, but the competition was fierce. I was up against Hudson Yang from *Fresh Off the Boat* and Marcus Scribner, Marsai Martin, and Miles Brown from *Black-ish*. Marcus won. It would have been nice to win, but I was happy that one of my friends got it. And I was excited that the NAACP even considered me for the award. I am so grateful that my hard work and all the effort I make to

be a role model and put forward a positive image was recognized. And I like to dress up for the award shows. They're fun, and I get to see my friends. They are my favorite events.

That same year, I was recognized by *Time* magazine as being one of the thirty most influential teens. Wow! I was on the same list as actors Yara Shahidi, Amandla Stenberg, Jaden Smith; Sasha and Malia Obama; Olympic gymnasts Simone Biles and Laurie Hernandez; and human rights activist Malala Yousafzai. I didn't even realize that *Time* knew who I was.

Because I'm on social media so much, I was invited to present at the Shorty Awards for people who produce short-form content, like on YouTube, Twitter, and Instagram.

"And the nominees are . . ."

For the first time ever, I was the presenter!

Whether I'm being nominated for an award or getting to be a presenter, it's really exciting to step into this new phase of my life—life after the amazing experience I had at Disney!

Now that my time on *Jessie* and *Bunk'd* is over, I have more time to spend going to auditions, thinking about what's next, and considering who I want to be during the next phase of my life, as well as far into my adulthood.

Not so long ago, I was that little girl fantasizing about coming to Los

Angeles to become an actor. I can hardly believe I've already accomplished so much. What do I dream about now?

Now that my life is like a clear blue sky in front of me, I definitely hope that I am still acting in the future. When I become an adult, I'd like to do at least five films: a drama, horror, thriller, action, even comedy—I would love to do all of it. I want to try every aspect of acting.

About a year ago, I started taking lessons to help me become a better actor. I'd never taken acting lessons in my whole life. I've gotten so far because I'm what they call a raw talent—acting came to me naturally. For a long time, I shied away from acting lessons because I thought only bad actresses needed them. Boy, was I wrong! Tom Cruise, Lupita Nyong'o, Viola Davis—everybody great takes them. There are some things you do just to better yourself.

I discovered that, because of all my years on Disney sitcoms, comedic acting comes more naturally for me. Now I find that I have to focus more and work harder on more dramatic roles. But I'm practicing and studying every day, and casting directors have said that I'm improving.

Acting lessons have been very helpful. Since I started taking them, I've tried new techniques like reading the whole script, rather than just my own character's lines and scenes. I always make sure to read the description of the character so I know more about them, how old they are, where they live, all of that.

Especially now that I'm older, I make sure to put my own life experience into my acting too. I do things like picture the scenes in my head and find my inner monologue, which is basically like having the same thought in your head before you say the line so it comes off as natural. Rather than blurting out a line I think of how I would say it in my head and really sink into it. I also make up the first part of the sentence in my head, but then only say my lines out loud. I've learned that acting is a lot like talking. I don't have to be as dramatic or put as much effort into it, unless I'm crying in a scene. I try to remember moments when I've experienced sadness and loss when I need to be emotional. These are things I didn't know how to do before.

♥

I am trying to be strategic about the roles I audition for. And even though I enjoyed playing her, Zuri is not who I am, so I don't want my next role to be a character who is a lot like Zuri. When I go to auditions, I don't try out for comedies, because I want to be seen as a girl who can act in dramas and thrillers, and someday romantic comedies. But these days, I don't get too upset with people for calling me Zuri. I *did* play her, and nine out of ten days, I loved it!

Going to auditions is an important part of acting. In this business, you have to have a thick skin. Recently somebody told me, "We loved you, and we thought you were the best for the part—but you're too short." They could have just kept that thought to themselves. But they didn't stop there. "You're so small—you're so cute," they told me. What they said made me feel bad for a minute, kind of like when I was a little kid

and got teased. I wanted to say, "Really?! What's your point? Because you could see my height from the information my manager sent you in advance."

Instead, I bit my tongue and said, "Yeah, I know I'm short. I see myself every day." I had to say something to stand up for myself, but I didn't want to burn my bridges. So I kept it at that. It's important that I just keep pushing and not let things like that get to me too much.

When I was younger, I used to hate being short, especially because I also look younger than I am. I would tell my mom that I'd rather be tall and look young or short and look old. My mom would say that being short is okay! Your height doesn't define who you are.

Maybe when I'm old I'll be glad I'm young-looking, but at sixteen, I'd rather look older. Fortunately, I've reached a point where I like my height. Every now and then, I wish I was taller, but this is how God made me. I've gotten used to it. There are a lot of short girls in the world, and there's nothing wrong with us.

It's just disappointing that casting directors and other people in the industry sometimes look at me differently because of my height. I can read a script and know, okay, I don't think they're looking for me.

There are times when you don't get a role because of things like your height, your weight, your skin color, you're supposed to be siblings but you don't look anything like the other character, how you read the role, someone else just read the part better, or your chemistry with the other actors—you get rejected for things like this frequently. Lots of times you never find out why. But I still go to the audition because it's good to be seen by different casting directors so they can remember me for the next role.

My mom taught me that something better will always come. Whenever I don't get a role, I really believe that something good will happen for me, so I don't stress too much. Even though I may want it, not every role is for me.

Also, in the future I hope to start directing and producing. In addition to being a challenge and a lot of fun, my appearance won't be as important if I'm working behind the scenes.

I've looked up to people like Raven-Symoné, Will Smith, and Tom Hanks, who have been in front of the camera but also direct and produce. They are behind some of your favorite movies, and sometimes you might not even know.

Leonardo DiCaprio is one of my favorite actors. I think he should have gotten an Oscar for *What's Eating Gilbert Grape*. He also produces a lot of good films. And you have to love Ava DuVernay, the first African American female director to be nominated for a Golden Globe and direct a film nominated for an Oscar for Best Picture. I think she's amazing. It's incredible to see all the films she has made, from *Selma* to *13th* to *A Wrinkle in Time,* and the lives she's impacted.

I'm watching their films, studying them, and then applying what I can learn from them in my life.

♥

I also want to continue my work in fashion. I already have my foot in the door, but hopefully I can take it to another level, where I can work with the bigger companies, like Puma or Tommy Hilfiger. It would also be great to do my own solo thing where it's my name, my brand, and I don't have to work for anyone—I work for myself. Like a lot of the kids of my generation, I hope to never have to work a regular nine-to-five job.

Ever since I was a young girl, I've stood up for what I believed in. Being an activist is not something I'm forced to do. I feel activism is so important, especially since social media can impact so many people. I will also probably become an animal-rights activist. I really love animals, and I especially love dogs. One day, I would like to own a big piece of land

where I can rescue dogs and bring them there so they can be free.

Activism will always be a big part of my life, and I will always stand up for what I believe in and what's important to me.

Sometimes I wonder if I will ever kick back in life. My friends tell me, "Oh, you're so famous. You do way more than I do." Even some of my friends who are well known—they work in music or are famous on social media—say the same thing to me.

But I always say I'm never satisfied with myself. So even if I have a

I WILL ALWAYS
STAND UP FOR WHAT
I BELIEVE IN AND WHAT'S
IMPORTANT TO ME.

TV show tomorrow, I'm not gonna be like, "All right, I'm good. I got a TV show." I'll keep striving for more. I feel like that's a good character-istic because it makes me want to work harder.

I tell myself, I've already made it so far at only sixteen. But I wanna keep pushing. And I know there are going to be setbacks in my life. But I know that I'm going to make it one day and will have the opportunity to do everything I want to do.

Finally, to all the brown-skinned girls. I appreciate you so much for all your love and support. The world may not always value you, but I love you and see you. I see your beautiful skin; I see your style; I see your amazing hair. Even if no one else understands the vision you have for your life, go for your dreams and don't let other people, no matter their color, get you down.

And as for my hair? Well, you can rest assured that you'll find it braided with extensions, or pulled back into a bun, or swept high on top of my curly head, or twisted out and floating free, just like my mom always wanted me to be.

Acknowledgments

I would like to thank God for giving me the life I have always dreamed of.

I want to thank Hilary Beard for taking this journey with me; my editor, Samantha Gentry, and the entire Random House team for giving me a platform to tell my story; and my book agent, Alyssa Reuben, for making one of my dreams come true.

To my father and my two little sisters—I hope you will learn a lot from this book.

To my best friends for always having my back and believing in me no matter what.

To my former teacher Cheryl Diamond, thank you for putting up with me for more than six years. You got me through most of my school years, and I learned a lot from you. I don't know how I would have survived those years without you.

To my current teacher, Kate Thompson, thank you for making my high school years a lot easier, and for sticking with me for more than five years. I am really going to miss you when I graduate high school.

Lastly, this book is dedicated to my mother. Thank you for giving up everything in your life so I could pursue my dreams to the fullest. I wouldn't be here without you.

Special thanks to my fans for everything you've done—I hope you all enjoy this book.

Photo Credits

ALEX.KRUK Photography: ii, 94, 133, 207; Barack Obama Presidential Library: 54, 55 (left); Bob Cass: 13; Chelsea Lauren: 148; Cheryl Diamond: 53, 107, 108, 109, 110, 111; Dascha Polanco: 154; DFree/Shutterstock: 118, © Disney Enterprises, Inc.: 32, 33, 55 (right), 80, 81, 82, 83; Evans Vestal Ward for Comic Relief USA: 147; Paul Smith for Featureflash Photo Agency/Shutterstock: 119; Josie Totah: 192; Kathy Hutchins/Shutterstock: 31, 37, 38, 72, 196, 198, 201, 202; lev radin/Shutterstock: 157; Lilly K Photography: 130; Ryan Bolton Photography: 74, 158, 159, 160, 161, 162, 164, 165, 168; Ryan Slack Photographs: 123, 124; Sara Cornthwaite: 151; Skai Jackson Family Collection: 1, 2, 3, 4, 5, 6, 7, 9, 11, 15, 19, 20, 21, 26, 34, 43, 45, 47, 48, 49, 50, 51, 52, 57, 58, 63, 67, 77, 85, 86, 87, 98, 99, 105, 114, 116, 125, 129, 132, 134, 145, 149, 150, 155, 167, 178, 181, 182, 183, 185, 186, 191, 203, 204; Decorative elements throughout © Shutterstock

About Skai

Skai Jackson is an actress and activist well-known for her roles on Disney Channel's *Bunk'd* and *Jessie*. She was named to the *Hollywood Reporter*'s Top 30 Stars Under Age 18 list, *Variety*'s Young Hollywood Impact Report, and *Time*'s 30 Most Influential Teens list, and was nominated for an NAACP Image Award. She's also been featured in articles in *The Cut, Teen Vogue,* and *Ebony,* among many others. She lives in Los Angeles. You can follow her on Instagram, Twitter, and Facebook.